PRAISE FOR *THREE BREATHS*

"In our fractured world, helping students find tools for peace, clarity, and compassion may be the greatest gift any educator could hope for. William Meyer offers a clear road map of realistic, accessible, and down-to-earth tools that can change young lives. Not only does *Three Breaths and Begin* provide clear guidelines for making meditation work in diverse classroom situations, it gets extra credit for its many stories, all shared with an engaging sense of authenticity, humility, and humor."

— **Donald Altman,** former monk, teacher, and author of
Reflect: Awaken to the Wisdom of the Here and Now
and *One-Minute Mindfulness*

"With engaging stories and heartfelt guidance, *Three Breaths and Begin* is a great resource for teachers who are considering bringing meditation into their classrooms. William Meyer demonstrates how silence can help young minds blossom."

— **Rick Heller,** author of *Secular Meditation:
32 Practices for Cultivating Inner Peace, Compassion, and Joy*

"*Three Breaths and Begin* is a truly unique guide to integrating meditation into every aspect of modern school life: taking tests, giving speeches, playing sports, going on field trips, and, when tragedy strikes any individual, bringing healing to the entire community. William Meyer offers a rare depth, breadth, and variety of practices for students to experience and reflect on, while addressing the very real concerns of teachers wanting to introduce practices that heal the mind and heart into standard curriculum. The wealth of inspiring stories from the classroom and the practical, down-to-earth specifics make this guide a worthy treasure."

— **Linda Graham, MFT,** author of *Resilience:
Powerful Practices for Bouncing Back from Disappointment,
Difficulty, and Even Disaster*

"I opened up *Three Breaths and Begin* in the middle of a snowy afternoon, and I did not put it down until long after nightfall. I was completely captivated by its beautiful and powerful message of connecting to our students not only with our minds but with our hearts as well. William Meyer's voice leads us in the direction of true enlightenment; with simple descriptions of his experiences both in and out of the classroom, he gently guides us to imagine ourselves as the compassionate mentors we know our students need and deserve. If you have ever wondered (even for a moment) if mindfulness practice has a place in the classroom, this is a *must-read*. And for anyone who craves a little beauty and hope in this ever-spinning world, pick up *Three Breaths and Begin* and enjoy!"

— **Jennifer Rosenzweig,** English teacher
and chair of the Student Wellness Committee
at Scarsdale High School, Scarsdale, New York

"*Three Breaths and Begin* is an invaluable resource for teachers, school psychologists, social workers, and guidance counselors to implement mindfulness in the classroom. As a school psychologist, I really appreciate how easy it is to pick up this book and incorporate the techniques. This book has various guided meditations that can be utilized in the classroom, in small groups, or individually with students. The format of the book as well as the content make it engaging for the reader to apply the skills. I highly recommend this book to anyone who is considering implementing mindfulness in a school or group setting."

— **Dr. Minu Thomas,** elementary school psychologist
at the Bronxville School, Bronxville, New York

THREE
BREATHS
And BEGIN

THREE
BREATHS
And BEGIN

A GUIDE TO MEDITATION
IN THE CLASSROOM

WILLIAM MEYER

New World Library
Novato, California

New World Library
14 Pamaron Way
Novato, California 94949

The material in this book is intended for education. It is not meant to take the place of diagnosis and treatment by a qualified medical practitioner or therapist. No expressed or implied guarantee of the effects of the use of the recommendations can be given or liability taken.

Text design by Tona Pearce Myers

Library of Congress Cataloging-in-Publication data is available.

First printing, April 2019
ISBN 978-1-60868-572-1
Ebook ISBN 978-1-60868-573-8
Printed in Canada on 100% postconsumer-waste recycled paper

 New World Library is proud to be a Gold Certified Environmentally Responsible Publisher. Publisher certification awarded by Green Press Initiative.

10   9   8   7   6   5   4   3   2   1

To my students, my teachers, and my family.
Thank you for showing me what it means to live,
love, and teach from the heart.

CONTENTS

INTRODUCTION

What do you think of when you hear the word *meditation*? Do you think of silence, crossing your legs, sitting in the lotus position, counting your breaths? All of these are small aspects of a complex and ancient practice, a practice that focuses on reconnecting with the self, directing the mind with intention, and awakening to a deeper awareness of the breath as well as the whole being.

I first became interested in meditation in the sixth grade after reading a book I found in the local library titled *Be Here Now* by Ram Dass (1971). After reading through this incredible work, I wanted to learn more about this practice, which promised euphoria, enlightenment, and a changed life. I suppose this is what every adolescent, as well as most adults, looks for in life: some type of transformation from the mundane to the extraordinary.

My uncle, a deacon in the Catholic Church, got wind of

my interest. He told me that he knew a Buddhist monk named Zahn Boh, and when he asked if I wanted to meet this person, I quickly agreed. One weekend during the school year, we headed down to Hamtramck, a diverse immigrant community on the east side of Detroit. After driving through a street lined with dilapidated buildings, my uncle parked his car in front of a house that was in disrepair. I hesitated. I wasn't sure if it was safe to get out of the car, but he reassured me that it would be all right.

We walked across the street and up the stairs to find, next to the front door, a sign on a small placard: "Zen Center of Detroit." We stepped inside, and there a young woman with a shaved head, dressed in gray robes, greeted us. My uncle told her we were there to meet Zahn Boh. She nodded, then led us up the stairs to the second floor and pointed toward another room. I followed behind my uncle into this small space, where to my surprise we found Zahn Boh sitting cross-legged on a cushion in deep meditation. Across from him were two more cushions. We sat on them and waited quietly for the attention of this middle-aged Zen master. Minutes passed — it felt like hours to my short attention span — before he finally opened his eyes.

I was at a complete loss for words. I didn't know how to greet a Buddhist monk. Do I bow, shake hands, smile? Fortunately, he was the first to break the silence. He looked at me with a piercing stare and said, "It has taken you hundreds of lives to sit on this mat before me."

I sat there, stunned by the monk's words. I'd never envisioned a life beyond this one, let alone hundreds of them. But something about his words resonated in my heart and gave an even deeper meaning to our encounter. The statement seemed to thrust me into the present moment in a way that I'd never before experienced. What followed was a lengthy conversation on mindfulness, Buddhism, and meditation. Although I can't remember the details of that conversation, or those of the many successive encounters with Zahn Boh, I do remember the feeling. The words he spoke, the way he poured the tea we drank, and the deliberate pauses between each of his breaths filled the room with peace and the power of living mindfully. I was instantly hooked.

After that first meeting, I began practicing meditation at night to help myself fall asleep. Then I began to use it before school, before my sports games, and even during my summer caddying job, until it just became an everyday part of my life. The ritual was simple. I would light a candle and place it on the floor, and then sit on a cushion. My only intention in those first few years was to follow my breath, calm my mind, and nurture a deeper sense of mental and emotional stillness. This practice stretched from six to seven minutes to longer periods in more troubling times. As my meditations deepened, I noticed the ripples from this practice spreading out across the rest of my day. There seemed to be more space in my life, more perfect timing, and a general sense of effortlessness. The days when I didn't meditate were chaotic, off rhythm, and simply a struggle. As I reflect back on my experience with the practice, I notice that during the stretches when I most needed meditation, I often abandoned it.

Today, I spend my days teaching history to adolescents in a high school just outside of New York City. As part of my pedagogical practice I meditate almost every morning. It is as important to my work as the lesson plan I drafted the night before or the cup of coffee I carry into school each morning. I find that meditation brings my life and my teaching into focus. It gives me access to clarity and insight. I can sense when a student isn't feeling well, and I have a greater empathetic capacity to sit with them and work through it. On a more basic level, students just appear when I need them, and my to-do list seems to take care of itself. And on the days I don't meditate, I still struggle to find my footing. I have less patience with my students, my peers, and especially myself. Meditation seems to bring the whole day into focus in a way that nothing else does, not even the coffee.

Since 2012 I have introduced meditation to my classroom as a tool to deal with the growing stresses of the school day, but also as a lens by which to facilitate greater connection between the students and the curriculum. What started out as part of a student research experiment involving a small group of six students sitting in the corner of a science classroom has grown into a club, a common occurrence in my classroom, and now an integral part of the community. As a result of the growth of this practice in the school over the years, students can be found meditating before tests, performances, speeches, sports games, and even assemblies. The meditation bug has not only bitten the students, but it has also caught the attention of the administration, faculty, and community. It has been incorporated into weekly department meetings and has become a part of professional development workshops, book studies, and even faculty wellness programs of the school. The parents have been equally enthusiastic, embracing meditation in the form of a weekly Thursday evening circle.

The breadth and variability of this ancient practice is what makes it so useful in schools. Whether a meditation is just a simple set of breaths before a major assignment or a longer visualization around a challenging personal issue, the flexibility of the form is what allows the whole community to access it wherever they stand (or in this case, sit).

OVERVIEW

This book is not an academic discourse on mindfulness or a psychologist's treatise on social-emotional learning; instead it's a teacher's perspective on the principles and practices of meditation and how they can be infused into the heart of the classroom. The purpose of this work is to show how meditation can help students better process their own lived experience so they may be more empathetic to others and of greater service to the world.

The first four chapters of the book open things up with a brief overview of the recent history of schools and the mindfulness movement, key tools for running a meditation, and finally the foundational components of space, silence, solitude, and story. The rest of the book looks at specific situations and strategies, such as leading meditations in high schools; starting clubs; meditating on field trips and with sports teams; meditating with younger students, teachers, and parents; dealing with tragedy; and implementing a meditation-centered curriculum.

Some of the chapters begin with or are centered on stories from my own experience. Traveling during the summer has helped me renew, recharge, and reconnect with myself as a teacher. I think, in many ways, it is in the act of disconnecting from the routines and rituals of the everyday that I suddenly connect to the extraordinary experiences and opportunities of the world around me. Drawing from some of those experiences and the inspiration they have provided serves as an entry point for several of the chapters that follow. While I hope that you find these stories engaging, I also hope they remind you of those personal and professional experiences that have enriched your own teaching.

At the end of each chapter I've also added a guided meditation. The majority of these are visual, while one or two focus specifically on breathing techniques and the use of silence. Like the opening stories in each chapter, I hope the meditations will provide a practical means to introduce one of the conceptual ideas and recommendations from the text. With the appropriate setup and timing, these meditations could be read as a script to a group of meditating students or simply as a guidepost of suggestions and imagery from which you can create and author your own meditations. There is no right or wrong way to use these scripts, as there is no right or wrong way to meditate. As I often joke with my students, as long as you are breathing you are doing it correctly. The most important attribute of a successful guided meditation is your level of comfort as the teacher. Trust your gut and the rest will take care of itself.

Although the underlying components of a successful meditation are fundamentally the same regardless of the context, the ins and outs of navigating disparate communities and implementing a guided meditation in a variety of situations require flexibility and a willingness to try new things. There are many forms of meditation, just like there are many different learning styles: auditory, visual, movement-based, and silent. Touching on a variety of these practices while helping students and teachers understand their own practice is a key element of this book. In some chapters I've even included student and adult reflections that I feel speak directly to the power of this practice.

By the end of this book, I hope you will have heard multiple voices and found useful activities for your classroom, tips for shifting the culture and space of your school, and lastly, guided meditations to use in your professional and personal practice wherever you might find yourself. I hope the stories in these pages also enrich your understanding, expand your curriculum, and awaken a sense of peace in your life. In whatever way this book speaks to you, may it be an invitation to a deeper conversation with your classes, as well as a more transformative experience for your students.

CHAPTER ONE

~~~~~~~~~~

HISTORY

One fall afternoon, when I was six years old, my grandfather came to my first-grade classroom to share stories and photographs from his recent trip to Egypt. He told many memorable stories from Egyptian history that day, but it was the one about the discovery of a young pharaoh's tomb in the Valley of the Kings that stuck in my mind.

My grandfather explained that at the turn of the twentieth century, Egyptologists had spent years exploring the valley, looking for the remains of any and every ruler they could find. By 1907 many had left the area, convinced that all of the major discoveries had already been made. One young British archaeologist, Howard Carter, was certain that a major discovery still remained to be made in the region. With the backing of a wealthy Englishman, Lord Carnarvon, Carter dug in the valley for more than a decade, interrupted for a time by the outbreak of the Great War in Europe. After the war he returned to Egypt and continued his expedition.

Four years passed, and Carter was no closer to making any new discoveries. Lord Carnarvon threatened to cut his funding if he didn't have something to show for his work. Then, just by chance, only a few weeks before he would have run out of money and returned to England in disgrace, Carter stumbled upon a single step, buried beneath the rubble of the valley floor. Soon his team started digging in the spot, and eventually they uncovered twelve more steps. At the bottom of this set of stairs was a sealed door. What followed would be one of the greatest archaeological discoveries in the history of the world.

As my grandfather described King Tut's tomb and the treasures Howard Carter unearthed that fateful November day, we all held our breath in anticipation of what might be found. Of course, we didn't understand the full significance of the discovery in either the history of Egypt or the history of the field of Egyptology. But we sensed that the opening of the tomb was not only a window into the life of an unknown boy pharaoh; it was also a window into a lost chapter of Egyptian history.

Like the discovery of that tomb, meditation is a doorway into a world of riches and treasures — not out in the deserts of Egypt, but right here within the center of our classrooms. For years now we have neglected many of the gifts and talents of the students around us, sometimes by choice but more often by the inability of our education system to understand how to engage more than just the mind. That deeper engagement is something the Egyptians, along with many other ancient peoples, recognized: the true power of the individual resides not in the head, but in the heart. In these next pages I hope to briefly outline the history that has shaped education policy in the United States, including the landscape of assessments that characterizes learning today. More importantly, this chapter will introduce the tools that mindfulness and meditation offer for uncovering the treasures beneath the surface of the mind.

EDUCATION HISTORY

As a high school history teacher, I often try to impress upon my students the importance of recognizing that history is not a static idea captured in a textbook, but a living and breathing entity that is constantly reshaping our lives. Over the past four decades, dating back to the publication of *A Nation at Risk*, in 1983, the US education system has witnessed an increased standardization of the K-12 curriculum. The focus of policy and teaching has moved away from the holistic, child-centered approach proposed[1] at the start of the twentieth century and instead turned toward one driven by the underlying desire to produce better and higher test scores.[2] Unfortunately, this movement has only accelerated in the past two decades, with a barrage of state and national exams ushered in through initiatives like No Child Left Behind (NCLB), Race to the Top,[3] and the more recent Common Core.[4] All this has left teachers as well as students lost in a barren landscape of testing and rote memorization.

As a result of all this assessment and policy shift, students have their minds stuffed with information but are rarely given opportunities for emotional or inner development.[5] Most teachers would agree that the result is high school graduates who are shortchanged and stilted — not just in their intellectual development but also in their emotional and inner capacities. Understanding the context of these reforms in the history of education and their consequences, both intended and unintended, is fundamental to understanding how we got where we are today, and how meditation can act in shifting that narrative.

ACCOUNTABILITY AND STANDARDIZATION VS. THE INNER LIFE OF THE CHILD

Few teachers would deny that students are constantly being overtested, overassessed, and overevaluated in a top-down effort to maximize performance and scores. Students no longer find themselves at the center of the classroom; rather, they are now secondary to the scores and numbers they produce. The result is more and louder calls for better results, more homework, and longer school years, all at the cost of meaningful and deeper learning.[6]

Recently, we've seen a wave of programs and trends challenging these forces. Some schools are introducing programs like mindfulness and yoga, and some are even reintroducing century-old electives on civic responsibility. Some students are being asked to explore deeper questions of who they are, who they want to be, and what they want to do. A larger part of this new movement is driven by concerns about student wellness and mental health that are ever more pervasive, with increasing self-reported rates of student stress, anxiety, and depression. Today we teachers find ourselves not just struggling to meet the demands of our administrators but often trying to navigate the mental health crises plaguing our students.

At the same time, mindfulness has become one of the most popular solutions to these problems. The first major effort to use mindfulness in the curriculum began in the United Kingdom in 2007. Since this initial project, interest in the movement has increased, and in 2015, plans to launch a seven-year $10 million study in the UK were announced.[7] The growing popularity of mindfulness has also taken off in the United States, where more than a dozen initiatives have been implemented, including MindUP and Mindful Schools. The Mindful Schools project has trained thousands of teachers and reached more than three hundred thousand students, most of them in California, New York, and Washington, DC. These programs have grown in popularity, especially among prestigious boarding schools throughout the Northeast. For example, Middlesex, a top prep school in Massachusetts, now requires all incoming freshmen to take a mindfulness course.[8]

A MIDDLE WAY FOR MINDFULNESS

With the efforts to introduce more mindfulness programming into the curriculum comes a counterwave of challenges and concerns. First, it is not uncommon to find that these potentially progressive reforms are being implemented piecemeal onto the mainstream curriculum.[9] Mindfulness programs or workshops on meditation are often offered as after-school programs or supplementary aspects of the school day. When they find their way into the curriculum, mindful practices of journaling, reflection, or moments of silence are rarely used as an integral part of the day. Even yoga is mostly included only as a part of physical education or as an after-school program.

Second, as currently applied, meditation and mindfulness have become seen as just another tool to increase teacher and student productivity, and thus they find themselves subject to the same external measurements they are attempting to challenge. Rather than using meditation as a force to initiate a deeper understanding of self, teachers have found that it has become just another skill subject to quantify, to increase productivity, or to improve behavior. These certainly are some of the positive attributes of the practice, and they shouldn't be taken lightly. But there is so much more that can be done with these tools, and much of their potential is currently being neglected.

For mindfulness or meditation to have value in many school districts, it must have proven scientific outcomes that lead to tangible academic results. This creates an inherent tension, as districts introduce these programs into the school day but rework them to remain subservient to the outcome model of education perpetuated by the mainstream. Meditation and yoga are then repackaged and justified for their benefits in terms of managing a classroom or improving test scores, but not for their capacity to prepare students for a more meaningful life defined by compassion, empathy, and inner exploration. We need a reimagining of meditation, one that doesn't force it into the current standards-based curriculum but rather honors its original intent and purpose of nurturing the heart as well as the mind.

Third, most of these initiatives and practices are being advocated by researchers, scholars, and administrators who stand outside the classroom door. Just as teachers who have little experience in the practice of meditation are ill-equipped to teach it to their students, the outside consultants who are encouraging its use are ill-equipped to recognize the unique needs of the classroom. A viable approach must be able to recognize the day-to-day needs and demands of the classroom teacher and take into account the myriad of forces constantly vying for their time. Consultants might be able to offer insights and new ways of thinking about mindfulness, but it is only a grassroots effort and classroom perspective that can truly comprehend and balance the pressures of the profession with the work of inner growth.

It is also important to note that meditation has been perceived by some as an Eastern religious practice. From the debate over prayer in the classroom to the current backlash around mindfulness, there is an ongoing battle wherever educators, parents, and politicians feel that a larger religious agenda is being pushed onto their children. These battles have played out in school board meetings, state legislatures, and even the Supreme Court.[10] Scholars and educators then struggle to find ways to explore the interior and inner life of students without framing it in a religious context. Meditation and mindfulness face this same challenge, as some communities feel they are advocating a specific form of non-Western prayer.

This book is not intended to advocate a spiritualized curriculum or specific religious tradition, but rather to explore how self-reflective habits of mind, like meditation, can be applied to the pedagogy and curriculum in a nonprescriptive or nonreligious way. I hope that this work, combined with the earlier research on social-emotional learning, mindfulness, service learning, and empathy, offers a promising pathway to the future. The current system — focused solely on external measures or the wholesale disregard of students' emotional development — is not a viable path forward, and yet one that completely drops testing and some measure of accountability isn't sustainable either. It is a matter not of one or the other, but rather of a middle way that can introduce meditation into the classroom while working in concert with the demands of the larger curriculum.

THE HEART

Modern conceptions of knowledge place great value on the head, or the intellect, but the sacred traditions of the ancient past situate this value within the heart.[11] This juxtaposition is worth noting since *mindfulness*, both as a practice and a term, is about the mind only, and many books about mindfulness are coming out of the fields of psychology and neuroscience.[12] This book seeks to look a little farther, to the connection between the mind and the heart, birthed from firsthand experience in the classroom.

What is the heart? The heart embodies the cultivation of values such as empathy, compassion, and service to the world, not just the maximization of student output or test scores. In seeking to understand the connection between the mind and the heart, this book explores meditation as a tool for helping students make meaning of their own lives and develop a deeper sense of self. In the process, some important questions are raised:

- How can educators broaden the curriculum to include the development of the student's interior life while also meeting the demands of today's standards-based curriculum?
- What does a curriculum that honors the student's inner life look like?
- How can meditation be incorporated so that it doesn't just compete but coexists with the current expectations of a standards-based model?
- How could principles of the practice of meditation help educators rethink teaching, the design of schools, and the design of professional development?
- Are there other modes by which the interior lives of students can be engaged that go beyond meditation?

By addressing these questions, we can shift the focus of educational theory and policy so that efforts to enrich the lives of students such as mindfulness and yoga are not lost in a wave of trendy reforms, becoming instead a lasting and transformative part of the curriculum. Exploring the inner aspects of a student's life through meditation might reveal a way to reintroduce these practices back into the curriculum in a meaningful way, not just as part of after-school programs, advisories, or electives.

RETHINKING THE CLASSROOM

When done well, meditation is a pathway to the heart. It offers an entry point into the most transformative parts of teaching, the parts where we engage with our highest selves. Today the benefits of these practices are well documented; one can find a thousand articles on the positive outcomes of teaching meditation and mindfulness to young people. But how to integrate them into a classroom remains unknown.

Here is a list of five simple suggestions that might help to lay the groundwork for meaningful student reflection discussed later in this book.

Less is more. Move away from the notion that more content is better, and instead create opportunities for students to engage with the material they are studying for extended periods of time and connect the material to their life. In contemplative practices this is called *rumination*.

Shift the focus away from outcomes. The more we gravitate toward test scores and end-of-year evaluations, the more we create a culture where the actual process of learning is being devalued. Redirecting student and teacher attention toward the wonder of learning is a must. Meditation can play a role in doing this by awakening creativity and curiosity.

Provide more opportunities for creativity and play. Whether it's as simple as letting a student choose the topic of a research paper or as artistic as replacing conventional modes of presenting knowledge with a visual display, let the students be creative. Creativity is a gateway to the inner passions and worlds that reside in the heart.

Bring back reading. Fewer and fewer high school students read for fun. Reading is probably the most important act students can engage in at any level to aid their cognitive growth and development. It not only helps foster a sense of curiosity and wonder, but it also reopens the mind to nonlinear ways of thinking that are integral to meditation. Reading is a foundational component of many contemplative traditions.

Get outside. Later I'll discuss the practice of meditation on field trips and in nature, but for now remember that simply getting students outside of the classroom and outside of themselves can be a powerful tool for accelerating their reconnection with authentic learning and reenergizing the room.

CONCLUSION

At this moment in educational history we have an opportunity to reevaluate not just what is being taught in the classroom, but how it is being taught. Placing our students' hearts at the center of the classroom is a radical act, one that has the potential to transform how we engage their whole lives, in turn transforming the type of people they become. The gateway to this transformation is meditation. Meditation is not an ending but a beginning, a doorway into the emotional and inner lives of our students. Shifting our attention and focus away from the head and the intellect to also include the emotions and the heart is crucial to a larger shift in schooling.

THE BREATH MEDITATION

Find a comfortable spot on a chair or cushion. Make any adjustments you might need, rotate your shoulders, relax your arms, and let your legs be loose. When you are ready, either lower your eyes into a soft forward gaze or, if you are comfortable doing so, close your eyes. Now take three breaths and begin.

Feel yourself breathing in and breathing out. Feel the space around you and within you.

As you take this next breath, let yourself go inward. Let go of the sounds around you, any other distractions, and gently move into a single-minded focus on your breath.

Imagine yourself at the doorway of your breath, that space where the breath enters and leaves. Just become an observer of that space. Feel the breath as it enters your mouth, your lungs, your chest, and your heart.

As you exhale, feel the breath leave from that same place and space. Pause. And then wait for the breath to return on the next inhale.

And then exhale, totally surrendering and letting go of the breath. And then come back to the inhale.

Let that inhale be the focus and focal point of your attention for the next few moments.

See if you can notice the place you first feel the warmth and air as it comes into your mouth or nose. See if you can notice the place where the breath last leaves. Again, if any distractions, thoughts, or feelings come up, just let them go, and come back to the breath.

See yourself as a gatekeeper, watching this door, this sacred space, where this life-giving force enters on the inhale.

Let the breath go, and as it leaves, release anything you want to let go — a test, a grade, a conversation.

As the breath comes back, let in only what you want to return. You are surrendering to what can't be held on to, and welcoming what comes back effortlessly.

Sit with this feeling for a minute, or several minutes, until you feel ready to move on.

And then, and only then, take three long breaths, focusing on the exhale, and when you reach the final one, open your eyes.

CHAPTER TWO

~~~ ~~~ ~~~

TOOLS

Immediately after college I had the opportunity to live in Prague for several months, teaching English. It was a short adventure, but one that had a huge impact on the direction of my professional life. While I was working through new classroom activities and unit plans, I would often take long afternoon walks through the city. I strolled along the Vltava River, across the Charles Bridge, and through the cobbled streets of the Old Town. It wasn't hard to imagine the medieval past in this place, with its astronomical clock and its towering church spires, and I could almost hear the thousands of footsteps that had preceded my own on these same narrow alleyways.

In the thirteenth and fourteenth centuries Prague was the center of the Bohemian Empire and the envy of the rest of Europe. Much of the beauty and wealth of this great city stemmed in part from Charles IV's enthusiastic patronage of the arts. Not only did he support hundreds of painters, sculptors, and architects, but he also let his wealth fund scientists, philosophers, and alchemists, who delved into the unknown and the mysteries of the world. The alchemists were unique. They weren't just seeking to understand the observable world; they were seeking ways to transform the interior and unseen world. For the alchemists it was about an inner discovery, a formula to transform ordinary stone into precious metal.

Seven hundred years later I found myself in the same city, making my own inner discovery. It didn't take long for me to realize that my strengths didn't reside in English grammar or punctuation rules, but in teaching. By the time I left Prague, my love for teaching was firmly rooted in my professional aspirations.

When I look back on my career, I have to smile because my teaching career and desire to uncover the hidden potential within each class began in a place where some of the greatest alchemists of the world once lived. As educators, we too are working with precious resources, except rather than looking for the elixir of life or transforming stone to gold, we search for passions and unseen talents. For me, meditation has been an invaluable tool in facilitating that deeper search and transformation. And like the alchemists, we need ingredients, formulas, and guidelines to help us in our quest.

TYPES OF MEDITATION

There are many different types of meditation, from walking meditations to guided meditations. This section describes some of the meditations touched on in this book. While these descriptions are brief, several types of meditation will be explained in more depth in later chapters, and some will be illustrated more fully with a guided meditation script. It is important to try as many types as you can and also to identify the ones you feel most comfortable with, as these are generally the best ones for you to lead. Each group of students is different, and what might work with one group won't resonate with another. You might surprise yourself with a little experimentation.

Meditations on the breath. One can do so much with the breath. Inviting students to breathe in through their nose and out through their mouth is a great way to calm the entire nervous system. Alternate nostril breathing — where students close one nostril with their finger and breathe exclusively through the other side, and then reverse this practice a moment later — helps engage both sides of the brain. And using the imagery of the ocean and waves coming up to the shore is also a powerful way to make students aware of their breath. As the waves mimic their own breathing pattern they can notice the depth of their breath, the speed, and the ease. If you do nothing but have your students focus on the breath, you will have introduced them to a powerful meditation practice.

Silent meditations. In these meditations you might begin with a few cues to re-center students, and then shift to a prolonged period of silence. If a practice of meditation has been well established with your students, silence can be a powerful tool. However, if they are new to meditation they might require more guidance, as this emptiness of noise and words might feel very unsettling, for both them and you.

Short meditations. This is a great practice before a test or a meeting: Have the whole group take three breaths, close their eyes, and count to ten in their head. You'd be surprised at what a dramatic shift takes place when you pause for just a few moments before beginning a task or a conversation.

Meditations on the body. These meditations are also known as *body scans.* After first starting with the breath, I often invite students to scan the body. You can start at the head or the toes; it doesn't matter. Just go slowly, and honor all sides of the body — left and right as well as front and back. A great deal of tension is stored in the joints and muscles. Just breathing into these areas can be healing.

Meditations on rooting. Rooting meditations are particularly useful during busy times of the year or stressful moments. I usually start a rooting meditation with the head and end at the feet. When students reach their feet, I have them imagine roots growing from the bottom of their feet or the tips of their toes. You can have them imagine these roots traveling as deep as you like, and even expelling the breath or negative energy down into the earth.

Meditations on the heart. This is one of my favorite meditations. After focusing on the breath and scanning the body, I then invite students to turn their eyes inward and follow their inhale into the heart. Provide the students with a specific image that they can imagine in that space: a room, a candle, even a flower. There are so many powerful images that can speak to a student's heart space. By *heart space* I mean the place where they feel most safe and comfortable in their lives. Letting them explore this imagery and check in on it over the course of multiple meditations can reveal so much about their emotional state, past and present.

Meditations on relationships. I engage in this type of meditation only when I have a very strong connection with the students. In this meditation, you guide the students into their heart space, and when they enter this space you might have them also invite in a friend, a family member, or someone else they have a close relationship with, living or deceased. When engaging in a meditation on relationships it is important that students feel safe and in control of the space. Many young people have experienced trauma that we as educators might not be aware of. If a student invites that trauma, or people connected with it, into their heart space without a support system, the meditation will be counterproductive and will harm them when it intends to heal them. I often use this meditation when working with adults, and parents in particular, as over the course of an adult life many close relationships may need healing.

Meditations on the curriculum. In these content-based meditations, students engage in a deeply visual and sensory practice where they actually see themselves being transported into the time or place of the topic they are studying. Several examples of student reflections on this type of meditation appear throughout this book. This type of meditation can lead to some startling discoveries. However, over the years I have learned that before starting the meditation, it's best to give students guiding questions that offer direction and purpose in their visualizations. Often I will then have students imagine doorways or labyrinths extending out from the heart space.

Meditations on the weather. These can be fun meditations with younger students, but I have also used them in Meditation Club, especially before big storms or possible snow days. Let the students imagine that their thoughts mirror the weather and play with that imagery as it passes through and out of their minds.

Meditations on energy. As I touched on earlier in this chapter, having students enter their heart space or scan their body and visualize a color can also be a great introduction to visualization. Once students get comfortable with this color imagery you might also ask them to use their inner eye to observe the color of their neighbor's energetic body (see "Energetic Body" on page 31). It is amazing to see how these colors change and shift through the year. This is also a great meditation for younger students.

GUIDELINES FOR MEDITATION IN THE CLASSROOM

Next I'd like to offer you some suggested guidelines for laying the groundwork for meditation and creating a transformative classroom experience. Please note, however, that like any lesson plan or initiative in the classroom, these are just suggestions that should never overshadow your own intuitive sense of your class. These ideas can provide a framework, but it is always the teacher's lived experience and the lived experience of the students that take priority. Many of these concepts will be discussed in even greater detail over the successive chapters, but for now here is an overview of fifteen key components.

Space. Creating space for meditation in the classroom is important to a successful practice and experience. Unfortunately, due to time and money constraints and an overwhelming desire for efficiency, we have neglected spaces for reflection in our schools. Desks are jammed into rooms to maximize the number of students one teacher can instruct, and budgets are redirected to accommodate the shifting trends in education. The result is a space crammed not only with furniture and people but with emotions, thoughts, and drama. There is little physical space for solitude, and in the midst of our efforts to maximize what is taught in the classroom, there are almost no moments of silence. This framing of classrooms and life leads students to feel anxious and overwhelmed. A reframing of the physical, intellectual, and emotional space of the classroom is the physical foundation to the conceptual principles of meditation.

Silence. An invaluable tool in deepening a meditation practice, silence can offer a little mental space in the constant clutter of thoughts and worries. It is so easy to introduce silence into the classroom, but at the same time, so disconcerting. As teachers we feel the need to fill every moment with our voice, tasks, and assignments, but sometimes just slowing the class down and pausing to reflect and think can be very powerful. Silence can be an equally effective tool when leading a meditation, even if it lasts only a few seconds or minutes. Allowing students that extra space is a gift that has been driven out of most classrooms today.

Solitude. There seems to be a real push within the classroom toward group work and group projects. This no doubt has its place in preparing students for many of the jobs and challenges of the world after school, but nurturing time and space where students can be alone with themselves is also important. When I take students outside the classroom and onto the front lawn or the back playing fields, I always encourage them to find a spot at least ten or fifteen feet from another student. Getting out of someone else's energy can free them to hear and connect with their inner thoughts. In the classroom it's usually not practical to create a separate physical space for each student. But even short moments for journaling or just sitting in silence offer students a valuable dose of solitude.

Timing. Creating more space in the classroom, whether for meditation, reflection, or silence, is also a question of time and timing. I think there are two ways to better facilitate this within the curriculum. First, I'd strongly suggest using the beginning of class for a written or reading activity that asks students to engage quietly with a text or prompt. The space created through this silent time can be cultivated and harvested later in the class for something much deeper.

For the last four years I've successfully taken down every clock in my classroom, much to the administration's chagrin. Not having a visible clock is a liberating experience for many students and helps to facilitate reflective spaces in the classroom. You can never go too deep in your conversations and meditations, but you *can* go too fast. If removing the clock is difficult, try just covering the face until after the reflection part of the meditation is over. Taking students "out of time" is one of the small cues, like putting the desks in a circle, that can really foster the intentionality of space needed for powerful reflection. The classroom should be a space both outside of time and outside of the constant technological buzzing that permeates the lives of so many young people.

Reflection. We might be tempted to skip this step, but it is worth your time to make sure students have space after a meditation to reflect on their experience, both privately in a journal format and publicly by sharing if they choose. Time can become such a stressor within the classroom, for both students and teachers. So it falls upon us as teachers to create spaces that stand outside of the schedule through our pedagogy and willingness to hear student voices.

At the end of all my meditations I have the students take a long exhale, wiggle their toes, and open their eyes. This simple ritual helps bring them back into their bodies, especially if the meditation had a visual or imaginative component. After the students have returned into their physical bodies, I then immediately have them journal or draw. Individual reflection gives students a moment to process their meditation: what they saw and what they felt. In writing these things down and sharing them, they might be struck by how their meditation was similar to others', or how it differed. This portion of the practice can last anywhere from one to fifteen minutes, depending on what the students are writing and how many of them share. The real benefits of meditation are not just in the personal practice but in the community it can help foster within the classroom.

Attention. *Attention* is a broad term that really drops into the heart of meditation. Many people assume that meditation is a very specific act involving a candle or a mantra. They might assume that in meditation one watches the breath or the thoughts of the mind. All of this is true, but there is no right or wrong way to meditate. Meditation is drawing the mind's attention to a specific task, thought, experience, or feeling. Today students are living lives at the opposite end of this spectrum, constantly being pulled in a million directions by social media, technology, and the drama of school. The goal of meditation is to draw the student's attention back to a singular point and in the process back into the present.

The Breath. There are many focal points for cultivating attention within students. The focus of attention could simply be the breath, a great starting point for any meditation. In this format, the student focuses on the inhale and exhale exclusively. When they notice that thoughts are distracting them from this focus, they come back to this simple practice. They might play with their breath, notice how it feels, observe the length, and so on, but the whole focus is the breath. This is often a great starting point for new meditators, but it is a great starting point for longer meditations as well. I almost always begin my meditations by having students really bring their attention to their breath. I find it is a way to draw them away from the outside world and into their own minds and hearts.

The Body. The body is an amazing tool for garnering the focus and the attention of students. Many young students unknowingly carry injuries, often the result of the hyperspecialization that has taken over sports in younger and younger age groups. Meditation can help reveal and heal these injuries and make students more aware of themselves as physical beings. An awareness of the physical body, starting with the head or the feet and then moving to each part of the body, can bring students into the present. When students discover an area that is particularly stiff or uncomfortable, simply invite them to breathe into this space. This act can serve not only as a healing balm, but also as a tangible place to direct their attention. As you move through the body it is sometimes fun to also ask students to notice how one side feels compared to the other. You can also ask them to explore any shifts they might notice in their body between the front and the back. Just as one might encourage students to play with alternate nostril breathing, an exploration of the sides of the body can be revealing as well.

Emotions. Our emotions are often directly tied to how we feel physically. When students identify feelings or areas of the body that are connected to those emotions, it can be very powerful, especially when they are unconsciously burying them. For example, a student who feels that they have to swallow their feelings or words around friends could discover discomfort in the stomach. A student having trouble standing up for themselves and expressing their ideas might feel pain in the lower back. And a student who is especially stressed or having trouble seeing an end to all their work might feel discomfort in the brow. Whatever the case, I always encourage students to

explore these spaces and breathe into them. It is not about trying to get rid of our emotions, but rather offering them space to
be. This is a great tool for all of us; often just a little space is all
we need to move through a particular feeling.

Energetic Body. I often direct students to focus on their energetic bodies. (While some teachers and students might have
trouble with this idea at first, it can become more easily ac-
cessed and visualized as one's meditation practice deepens.)
The energetic body is the body that surrounds one's physical
and emotional self. I encourage students to imagine a color for
this body, and oftentimes I even have them imagine the color of
the energetic bodies sitting next to them in the circle. As they
explore this visual, I then have them begin to move their awareness through the whole space. Are colors or energies that are
not their own present in the space? Are ideas or feelings that
are not their own stuck in their energetic body? It is amazing to
see what students find and discover through this practice. For
many young people, separating their own wants, desires, and
feelings from those of their teachers or their parents or their
peers can be very enlightening.

The Heart. Once we have explored the breath, the body, and
the energetic body, I then invite students to turn their mind's
eye inward, to drop into their heart. Here I encourage them to
shift their attention into an imaginary or creative world. This
doesn't mean that they cannot feel sensations in their body, but
it does mean that the focus of their attention will be visual imagery. This guided practice produces some of the most striking discoveries and insights in meditation. However, it should
be done only if all are comfortable and safe. Throughout this
book you will find images and symbols that I draw upon when
leading students into the heart, including labyrinths, circles,

and images from nature. Feel free to use these in your own practices.

Sharing. Obviously you never want to pressure a student into sharing something, but creating the space and the time for sharing is so important. This is where a meditation shifts from a solitary experience to a communal one. There is power in numbers, and there is power in sharing a meditative experience. Countless times I have been amazed to see how one student's meditation experience, initially seeming incomplete to them, becomes clearer after hearing about another student's meditation. In some cases, it is like watching a jigsaw puzzle of stories come together, creating an even more expansive and visually stunning whole. In so many ways this final act is what really deepens the experience and grows the community.

Listening. I recently came across an article describing poor communication between doctors and patients. It cited one study that looked at how long it took a doctor to stop listening to their patients and interrupt. The answer: eighteen seconds.[1] I would be curious to see how a similar study would play out in a classroom. It wouldn't be surprising to find that teachers are also guilty of rushing to conclusions, limiting student responses, and at the deepest level, preventing students from telling their stories. We do this in so many ways, some conscious and some unconscious. Often we cut students off so we can race forward in the curriculum, and it is the rare exception that students are able to share their experiences on a deeper level. Listening is an active part of being present, not a passive one. We need to learn to listen to ourselves, to others, and to the world around us. After meditation, holding space for another and hearing them in our hearts is a gift. However, this gift is available only if we are present.

Voice. Finding your voice is a huge part of running success-ful meditations. Whether it is the volume of your voice, or its timing, or just how it expresses confidence, your voice is a tool in leading students in their meditation practice. Think about the power of your voice and how it is used. Pay attention to the people around you and how their voice affects others. Is it grating to the ears? Is it piercing, strong, or overwhelming? Or is it gentle and kind? When you lead a meditation you lead it with your voice, but you want it to be connected to your heart. The voice needs to be clear and strong, but it never should feel commanding or demanding. It should not control, but guide, offering a constant invitation into the student's inner world and mind. Over the years I have found a softer voice in my medita-tions, one that is nurtured by the space between my words, not necessarily the volume or intensity of what I say.

Pacing. Finding the right pacing for my meditations with students and teachers was tricky at first. I couldn't gauge whether I was going too fast or too slow, if I was losing my audience or rushing them through their experience. Today, I have slowed my narration dramatically. I find that less is more, and that just a word here, or a reminder there, goes a long way when students are turning their attention inward. Talking slowly can be an adjustment both for them as listeners and for you as the speaker, but in general after a minute or two a shift will occur in the room and everyone will begin to settle down. I also find it helpful to give meditators an extra minute before I transition from breath to body or from body to imagery. You will be surprised at how much bubbles to the surface when stu-dents begin to meditate, and you will want to give them the op-portunity to process those experiences. If nothing else, a slower pace allows the students to breathe, literally and figuratively, in an environment where they aren't constantly being inundated with information and instruction.

CONCLUSION

The alchemists of old have become the teachers of today. Classroom instruction is transformative in a way that is unlike any other experience or space in our modern world. Often we as teachers find ourselves spending more time with students over the nine to ten months of the school year than we do with close members of our family. Meditation is an invaluable tool to deepen those bonds and facilitate that alchemical transformation.

THE HOUSE MEDITATION (BODY SCAN)

Find a comfortable spot on a chair or cushion. I ask you not to cross your arms or your legs. It's best if you just place your hands softly on your thighs, or wherever may be most comfortable. When you are ready, either lower your eyes and just stare with a soft gaze at the floor or the desk, or if you are comfortable doing so, close your eyes. Take three breaths and begin.

Visualize yourself at the threshold of your breath. Let the breath draw you inward as the breath enters. Release the outside world, the sounds, the thoughts, the people. Let all that go as the breath leaves.

Let the breath find its own balance, rhythm, and ease. Let any heaviness or stickiness leave you as you exhale, and let light fill you as you inhale. As you become more comfortable with your breath, imagine your gaze shifting inward.

With each breath imagine yourself traveling through the home of your body.

First imagine the breath traveling into your mind, that attic of your being. Notice what's in that space — any clutter, old ideas, or forgotten treasures — and let the breath move through it, reconnecting with what was forgotten, or clearing what needs to be removed.

Take another breath and feel it move down through the wings of your home, your shoulders, your arms, and your fingers. Notice what you want to release, and just let it go out the doorways of your fingertips as you exhale.

Take another breath, and this time feel it in your

heart, the center of your home and being. Notice the emotions, feelings, and joys you hold in there. Again, just watch anything you want to let go of leave out the door.

Take another breath and move even deeper. Feel the breath moving into your core, the hearth of your house. Here you may find stickiness, heated emotions, or ideas that no longer serve you; just let those go.

When you are ready, take one more deep, full breath and feel your connection with the earth. Feel your feet and point of contact with the ground. Notice anything that may be causing cracks in your foundation, like doubts or second-guessing. Let the breath move through here — let it clean and clear — and then let it go.

As you take the next breath, feel the windows of your being open. Feel the breath move in every direction through your heart, your body, and your mind.

Let the breath open and release out of every pore and cell of your body.

And then when you are ready, but only when you are ready, take one more breath and gently open your eyes.

CHAPTER THREE

⧉⧉⧉

SPACE

Several summers ago my wife and I had the opportunity to travel through northern France. It was a breathtaking trip. We saw the Bayeux Tapestry, traveled to the beaches of Normandy, walked the steps up to the top of Mont-Saint-Michel, and trekked through the alignments in Carnac. Each of these places held a magical energy. From the haunting stillness of the American cemetery standing guard above Omaha Beach to the magical alleyways and stone steps leading to the top of the abbey on Mont-Saint-Michel, it all spoke of another time and another world. But one particular stop at the end of our trip profoundly transformed my own understanding of space and the sacred.

As a historian, I could say so much about Chartres, and it will be revisited many times in this book. The structure was built and rebuilt in the thirteenth century around a single garment, believed to be the tunic worn by the Virgin Mary while giving birth to Jesus. This single piece of cloth has drawn thousands of pilgrims to the cathedral steps each year, including kings, queens, popes, and prime ministers. Within the cathedral are equally breathtaking pieces, like the incredible collection of stained-glass windows that adorn the walls, monuments to the architectural alchemists of the medieval world.

For now, though, I will point out only three things about Chartres: the labyrinth, the well, and the windows. Each of these is more striking than the next. The labyrinth is a kind of maze in the center of the cathedral used for prayer and meditation, laid into the stonework of the floor and walked at specific times and on certain holy days of the Church year. The well, connected to an ancient Druidic spring associated with healing, resides in the crypt and descends about fifty meters into the earth. And the stained-glass windows, created as a symbol of the divine, illuminate the interior with images of light and color. As my wife and I explored the cathedral, I marveled at the magic of this space. I felt the innate pull of everything drawing me inward. Like the labyrinth that leads to the center, the well that is dug deep into the earth, or the windows that transform the ordinary light of the exterior to the transformative light of the interior, everything about Chartres led me into deep inner reflection.

SACRED SPACE

Creating sacred spaces has always been part of the human desire to build. Whether it was stone circles in the fields of England or the pyramids on the Giza Plateau, humans have sought to create spaces that inspire creativity, connection, and a calling to our highest selves. Chartres is not unique in its power to inspire a movement inward, but as a totality it is unique in the explicit manner in which it conveys this message.

The labyrinth is one example. While the labyrinths of other cathedrals were destroyed, the Chartres labyrinth became more and more popular, creating a place and space within the collective consciousness that couldn't be destroyed. Today the Chartres labyrinth has been replicated thousands of times, outside of churches, in fields, and even on the greens of college campuses. There is a deep human desire to move inward and to explore the remotest parts of ourselves, something the labyrinth facilitates. As teachers we also have the potential and power to inspire that same sense of wonder and awe within our students.

At the start of each year I always take a day or two to explore the spaces where I'll be teaching. It is crucial for me to set foot in those rooms before my students do, to see the arrangement of desks, to notice the way the light enters in the afternoon, and to set an energy across the whole area. Creating an intentional physical space is the first step to creating a space for interior exploration. Just as I would set up a meditation corner within my own home, creating a space for reflection in the classroom ahead of time helps me to lead a successful meditation practice throughout the year.

There are always limitations to the spaces we are given as teachers, which might include a room's small size or having to share space with another teacher. For this reason, trying to find ways to use the space creatively, as a tool in building community rather than as an obstacle, is crucial. Whenever setting up a room, I try to maximize the number of desks that face each other. Circle, horseshoe, or amphitheater arrangements are some of my favorites. I almost always place my desk on the outside of this circle and in a position where it can face the door.

I also like to bring life and color into the room. Rather than leaving the walls blank, I try to hang a collection of student work from over the years, as well as objects of meaning from my own experiences. The classroom then becomes a gallery of student artifacts as well as an outer reflection of the inner world I hope to cultivate. A plant is also a great addition to a corner of the room (which could also serve as a dedicated meditation corner), bringing a little more life and clean air into the space. I also keep a meditation bell on my desk and drape prayer flags along the back wall. Unfortunately, as a high school teacher I don't always get to stay in the same room throughout the year, but even when I move around these little objects give students a hint of what is to come.

GREETINGS AND GROUNDWORK

After you take the time to create a sacred space in your classroom, don't be afraid to make changes. Just as I might change a student's seating assignment, throughout the year I often revisit the classroom space I've created, looking over the desks and chairs and thinking about how well the arrangement serves my students, as well as my intentions. Space has a huge impact on experience, and taking the time to create and improve that space with intentionality is crucial to teaching at all levels.

Even if it might mean starting a few minutes late, I will hold students outside the room so that I can clean up from the previous class, both physically (pushing in chairs and picking up papers) and energetically (opening a window and raising a blind). Clearing old energy or thoughts before inviting a new class in is an easily overlooked act of teaching. When students do finally enter the room, I make sure to greet them at the door.

This is an old trick, dating back to my first days as a teacher in the classroom. As they enter, I look each one in the eyes, shake their hand, and create an immediate connection. This not only sets the tone but also gives me an opportunity to really see each student and do a quick assessment. If I notice that a student looks distracted or upset, I might pull them aside to talk, or get their attention at the end of class.

The groundwork of creating the classroom space before students arrive supports the opportunity for meditation at any time during the year. Deep reflection won't happen by chance, without an environment where students feel safe, supported, and seen. Teachers are often surprised when students seem disengaged from the class material or to lack interest in anything at all. The same teachers may even wonder why they are unable to get to the depth they desire in their meditations with students. However, until students feel a personal connection to the teacher, it is unlikely that they will invest in the class and even less likely that they will feel comfortable enough to move deeply into a meditation.

Meditation won't fix lingering disciplinary problems within the classroom. In fact, existing issues are often deepened by classroom meditation. You will meet significant obstacles if students don't feel that you control the space enough for them to let go in it. If the classroom is a space of openness, respect, and honesty, a well-timed meditation can deepen the connections among students, as well as connections between students and teacher, in unexpected ways. However, if teachers expect a meditation to solve a persistent classroom problem or persistent disruptive behavior, they must be warned that such an inner practice might open something even more problematic or unexpected in a class.

Unless face-to-face interaction would be unsettling, I always recommend seating students in a circle. I'd also remove any desks from the equation if possible and have the students bring their chairs and notebooks for writing and reflection to the center of the vortex. Allowing students to participate in the creation of this space simply by moving their desks can be a wonderful tool in helping them prepare for the meditation. The physical arrangement of the classroom unconsciously triggers an inner shift in awareness: this is not just another class activity or simulation. You can do this for any lesson; whenever you are looking to shift the energy of the room, just change the layout.

Once the space is created, then you can begin a meditation.

SHIFTING FROM SPACE TO MEDITATION

When meditation is done well, it can open up spaces within the student for insightful and transformative reflection. I would not recommend expecting this type of experience the first time you sit down with your class, but over time and with intention, the results will surpass even your wildest imaginings. Below is a particularly powerful student reflection written after the final visual meditation of the year. The students were led in guided meditation, using the theme of circles and connection, in which members of their family were imagined into the experience. Here is what my student Lain Miller experienced, as described in her post-meditation reflection:

> The meditation began with my younger sister, my dog, and I running through a grassy meadow in springtime. My sister and I were wearing pink and white dresses, which matched the petals of the flower tree we lay

down under. The petals then began to fall around us in a perfect circle. I believe the pink in our dresses and flowers as well as our dog is meant to symbolize youth, while the white in our dresses, the flowers, and the season is meant to represent rebirth. We then stood up and the flowers around us began to swirl until we were enclosed in a tornado of petals. Then the petals dropped to the grass, all at once, once again in a perfect circle....

Then the petals repeated their swirl, dropped, and we saw our ancestors. At this point I saw a man dressed in a silver chest pad with three circles, a red shirt, and a fluffy red and black hat. He almost looked Russian, or like a member of the Golden Horde to me. I then asked him, "Are you the warrior I am descended from?" as my name means "descendant of a warrior." He replied, saying, "We are not warriors, we are protectors of knowledge." I then came back to the center of the circle, where I saw my sister talking to a Native American warrior with similar symbols painted in a red war paint across his body. But she said nothing of it.

Lain Miller

May 16, 2014

Lain's story, while laced with extraordinary imagery and poetic connection, was not unique. Her description seems to capture the transformative potential of this type of reflection in helping to bring meaning and sense-making to the roles different individuals play in our lives. What I also love about Lain's piece is the way in which she also reenvisions the traditional role of the professor and the historian — from passive observer to active warrior, guarding the treasures of the past. The reframing of experience and the garnering of wisdom from what can sometimes be considered challenging is an outgrowth of meditation.

MONET AND L'ORANGERIE

The same summer my wife and I discovered Chartres, we found another place that reminded me of the need for reflection and stillness. A former *orangerie*, or citrus tree garden, it is located in the center of Paris not far away from Chartres, in the southwest corner of the Jardin des Tuileries. Only a short walk from its bigger and older sibling, the Louvre, l'Orangerie became a museum in 1851. For seventy years this little museum went unnoticed, and on more than one occasion it was almost closed. Today the museum offers a fabulous concentration of masterpieces by Cézanne, Renoir, Picasso, Rousseau, and Matisse.

The transformation of this little building and the space within began at the start of the twentieth century, when one artist, Claude Monet, sought to display some of his most powerful works there. Monet was one of the fathers of the impressionist movement and an alchemist of his world. His paintings offered a new perception, one that looked to capture color and light. He painted everything from sailboats to cathedrals, but his greatest achievement would take place in the back of his small Giverny farmhouse. Monet spent the majority of his life painting the water lilies that floated on the surface of his small pond. These objects became his obsession until his life was transformed by a war that consumed Europe.

The Great War highlighted the best and worst of humanity. For four years it ravaged the countryside of northern France and destroyed the lives of many, including Monet's friends and his family. Seeking some solace in this incredible time, he poured himself into his painting. At the end of the war, Monet offered to the French government a series of paintings the like of which had never been seen, eight giant murals capturing the beauty of his treasured water lilies in vivid detail. The home for his murals would be l'Orangerie.

Walking into the circular rooms in which the paintings are hung, I was struck by these works and how they reminded me of Chartres Cathedral. Monet's gift to France was a gift to the world. Through his painting and the design of their display, Monet created a space for peace and reflection at a time of turmoil and uncertainty. He understood well that it is only from the center of the room that you can see the full beauty of these paintings, and it is only from one's heart that we are able to appreciate the beauty and love within life.

TIPS FOR CREATING A MEDITATION SPACE IN THE CLASSROOM

The anonymous engineers and designers of Chartres Cathedral understood that the symbol of the labyrinth could be an invitation to go inward, Claude Monet recognized that a circle could offer a space of refuge in the midst of a world of chaos, and as teachers we have the power to create a physical space within our classrooms that reconnects students to their highest selves. Here I'd like to offer a few suggestions to help you design the space for your classroom meditation.

Clear the room. Take time between all classes, but especially before a class you intend to meditate with, to clear the room of the energy from the previous class. Letting everyone out of the room, taking a breath or two, and then letting the next class in can be a reenergizing practice.

Meditate in circles. I always use the circle when leading a meditation, whether it's in the classroom or outside on the grass. This simple but powerful form allows for a deep sense of community and clear lines of sight between you and all of your students. And no matter how long it might take to re-arrange the room, I have found the creation of the circle to be a powerful tool for enhancing the collective experience of the meditation. So impressed have I been by the effectiveness of this formation that I now often find myself using it to facilitate other classroom activities as well.

Position yourself in the seat closest to the door when leading meditation. This is a great strategy, especially when there is noise in the hall. Your back serves as a human shield, and it allows you to better project your voice into the room over the sound of outside noises.

Turn off the phones. You should always remind students to turn off their phones. Nothing is more disruptive in a medita-tion than the constant buzzing of a group text or random phone call. I'd also try to turn off the ringer of the class phone, if pos-sible. (Check with your administration before doing this.) It is nice to have a quiet space, even if just for a few minutes.

Hang a sign on the door. After the desks have been ar-ranged in a circle and students have found their seats, I walk to the door and put up an outward-facing sign that reads "Quiet Please, Meditation in Progress." There are so many unexpected interruptions in the course of the school day, and this can be a simple way to cue outsiders not to disturb you.

Hang quotes on the walls. Among your wall art, include quotes from thinkers like Thoreau, Gandhi, or Dorothy Day. These can be nice reminders of the tenor and purpose of the space. These quotations don't have to be religious; in fact, they probably shouldn't be.

CONCLUSION

While my love for history comes out in my teaching every day, to me, the real purpose of the classroom is to guide students to the teacher within themselves. Empowering them to be authors of their own lives and to write their own destinies is an invaluable gift. It is not just about dumping content into a student's head; it is about awakening something within their hearts. When the physical space is created, the exploration of the interior will effortlessly follow.

THE ROOTING MEDITATION

Find a comfortable position on a chair or cushion. I ask you not to cross your arms or your legs. It's best if you just place your hands softly on your legs, or wherever may be most comfortable. When you are ready, lower your eyes and just stare with a soft gaze at the floor or the desk or, if you are comfortable doing so, close your eyes.

When you are ready, take three breaths and begin.

With each breath, breathe deeper into yourself. Feel the air filling your lungs — the top, the back, and the bottom.

Begin to move your attention with this next breath into your heart center. Feel that space, that warmth, that presence.

Take another deep breath and imagine there is a small point of light in your heart center.

Give that light a color, imagining that this light represents your most authentic self.

As you breathe, you can feel yourself moving closer to that light and that light growing stronger in your heart center; it grows brighter, stronger, warmer.

All the while you are continuing to breathe, feeling a deeper sense of presence and peace.

Take another breath and feel your energy and focus move down your spine to the base of your feet. This is your connection to the earth.

Take another deep breath and feel that space at the base of your spine and feet open. Imagine roots growing down into the ground as you breathe in through your mouth and exhale out through your feet. With each breath let your roots go deeper and deeper

— through the topsoil, the bedrock, all the way down to the center of the earth, making a firm connection between you and the planet.

Take another breath, and bring yourself again to your heart center.

Emotions might pass through your mind and heart, but that's all they will do. They are like clouds moving across the sky, while you are firmly rooted. In this position, check in with how you feel. Do you feel tension in your body? Make no judgment, just feel.

On this next breath imagine any tension or pain, any unwanted energy, running down your spine and legs into the earth.

Take another deep breath and continue to release any tension, any fear. You can let all that go. All the while, you continue to breathe and to center yourself on your heart as the flood of light there opens.

Now begin to move your attention and breath down to your feet. Imagine you are bringing in a light up from the earth, through the soles of your feet. This light travels up and out of your mouth. You can give it a new color.

Feel the light continue to rise through your feet, your ankles, your knees, your hips, your lungs, your heart, and overflowing into your arms, your fingers. With one deep inhale feel it rise up through the crown of your head.

Like a tree in springtime, feel yourself blooming, growing, and embracing the world.

And then, and only then, take three long breaths, focusing on the exhale, and when you reach the final one, open your eyes.

CHAPTER FOUR

೬ⵜⵝⵙ ೬ⵜⵝⵙ ೬ⵜⵝⵙ

SILENCE AND SOLITUDE

Chapter 3 was all about the physical space needed to meditate, and this chapter explores the inner space. Exploring the inner landscape of the heart requires us to shape not only the outer space but also the mental and emotional space. This shaping is made possible by many factors and forces at work in the lives of young people; among these, silence and solitude are two ingredients. Unfortunately, in this outcome-driven world, we neglect these two aspects more than any other area of the classroom.

When many of us think about silence and solitude, we are reminded of the medieval monks or mountain hermits from another era. However, this couldn't be further from the truth. As two modern monastics revealed, the presence of silence and solitude, as well as the act of moving inward, is what prepares us for better serving our schools and our communities.

THOMAS MERTON AND THICH NHAT HANH

Almost fifty years ago, two monks, Thomas Merton and Thich Nhat Hanh, one Christian, the other Buddhist, were drawn together by their opposition to the war in Vietnam. Their meeting, arranged by the Fellowship of Reconciliation, an international pacifist organization to which both men belonged, was an opportunity to share their perspectives on this conflict and in the process to open an East-West dialogue between two different, but complementary worldviews. In this conversation, they discovered the common roots of their faiths in an underlying monastic tradition and a shared desire for greater compassion, self-reflection, and love throughout the world. And while these two men met only once, at the Gethsemani Abbey in Kentucky on May 26, 1966, together their philosophies on solitude, silence, and contemplation transformed the lives of millions.

Contemplation

Contemplative thinking, or intentional reflection for an extended period of time on a particular issue, thought, or emotion, stands upon the groundwork of silence and solitude. Merton, a graduate of Columbia University who became a Trappist monk, understood that even in the 1930s, the ever-growing speed and sound of the modern world was destroying humanity's connection to the heart. Often in his writing he lamented the lack of space for individuals in their quest for greater inner fulfillment. He was drawn to a life of solitude and silence as a means to understand what he described as his true self.[1] Much of his later writing built on these same notions and reinforced the need for greater silence in the modern world.

Vietnamese Buddhist monk Thich Nhat Hanh — called Thay, or *teacher*, by his followers — advocated for silence, recommending in his many writings and talks that we find moments of silence and stillness throughout the day through the practice of mindfulness. Rather than isolating oneself from the daily grind, he encourages a deeper engagement with and awareness of the everyday occurrences in life through mindfulness. Thich Nhat Hanh's teachings have had far-reaching impact. He has been a powerful proponent of meditation; prior to his writing on the subject, meditation was a mystical practice reserved primarily for monks. Today, meditation is accessible to people of all age groups.

One of Thich Nhat Hanh's key teachings focuses on the power of silence: it is through silence and out of meditation that we might address the world's larger social problems. We teachers can thus use meditation as a tool of civic education, empowering our students to engage with the wider world as well as with the daily dramas of the classroom. Meditation helps students to recognize the interconnectedness of all life, and this allows them to look beyond their own pain and suffering and to recognize the pain and suffering of others, including the pain they themselves are inflicting.

Education, then, represents an axis point for the synthesis and application of these powerful ideas. The challenge is summarized by these questions:

- How does one take the practice of silence and solitude found in monastic settings and explore its relevance to schools in a complex, interconnected, and noisy world?
- How does one understand the practice of silence

and solitude as understood through the monastic
experience?

- How is the monastic experience of silence and solitude relevant to learning in the public setting of
the school?

Human-centric Curriculum

A missing piece in today's conversation about schools and education is the direct application of a *holistic curriculum*. By this I
mean a curriculum that acknowledges the emotional and inner
lives of students, not just obsessing over the accumulation
of facts within their minds. Looking at the work of Thomas
Merton and Thich Nhat Hanh in the field of contemplative living and learning, one can see a new (or rather an old) perspective for studying classrooms in the twenty-first century.

Merton and Thich Nhat Hanh offer a path back to a holistic
curriculum. In both Eastern and Western contemplative traditions there is a foundational element of silence and solitude, as
well as the space for students to reflect and move inward. These
two ingredients are key factors, not just in transforming the
space of a classroom but also in inviting students deeper into
themselves. When the classroom is filled with constant noise,
activities, and at times distractions, there is no space for us to
think, let alone feel.

GREAT SILENCE

In 2007, the film *Into Great Silence*[2] was released. By the Ger-
man director Philip Gröning, the movie was based on a simple
idea: Gröning wanted to capture the life of a community of
Carthusian monks living in the Grande Chartreuse, one of the

most remote monasteries in the Western world, nestled high in the French Alps.

Gröning first had the idea for the film in 1984. When he approached the monastery's abbot with a request to make the documentary, the abbot declined, citing the need for further reflection and time to think about it. Sixteen years later, an unexpected letter appeared in Gröning's mailbox; the abbot was inquiring whether he was still interested in the project. It required six months of filming with no outside light and no outside support for Gröning to capture the images he sought, and then another two years of editing before the film was released. Dating from Gröning's initial request, the film took over eighteen years to make. In the end, at two hours and forty-nine minutes, the film had no spoken commentary and no added sound effects, and it captured the heart and silence of this remote monastic community.

Over the years I have shown clips from this movie in my ninth-grade World History course. Each time I show it I'm struck by how deafening the sound of silence is to the ears of overscheduled and overstimulated teenagers. It takes them more than a few minutes to adjust to both the pace and the stillness of the film. I share this because it is well worth taking this kind of progressive dip into the waters of silence, in a non-meditative state, before introducing students to a deeper meditative practice. Even simple reading activities or personal writing explorations, with intentional periods of silence, can serve the same purpose.

Most days I begin my classes with a writing assignment. I find that this serves to reset the classroom tone by clearing whatever emotional baggage the students have brought into the class and calming the waters of their busy minds. Some teachers use a meditation bell to open class, but for me writing is simpler and more conventional pedagogically. Whatever practices you choose, your willingness to sit with unanswered questions and the general space of quieting the room are key to later meditation success. The waters must first be still before one can see into the depths.

Silence also creates the space for deep listening to both others and the self. Thich Nhat Hanh calls this *compassionate listening*. When we really listen to someone, when we create a space for them to tell their story, it is an act of healing. So much disease and anxiety is caused by holding on to things. Compassionate listening allows for the sharing of emotions, and it is transformative for both the listener and the speaker. Deep, lengthy unburdening isn't always necessary. Simple things like sharing a smile, offering a laugh, or creating a sense of ease with your students can help them feel cared for and seen. In the classroom, the first contact begins when a student first enters your presence, not when they open their mouth. Recognizing each student from the first moment with simple acts and gestures nurtures the level of comfort and security they need to feel to be willing to let go.

ENGAGED CONTEMPLATION

Thich Nhat Hanh, unlike Merton, was an actively engaged contemplative early on in his spiritual life. The Vietnam War, which destroyed his homeland, made politics and the problems of the world an unavoidable reality. So he focused on applying his training as a Buddhist monk to help ease the pain and suffering everywhere around him. He created the School of Youth for Social Service, founded the Hungry Children Project, and wrote letters to key leaders, like Martin Luther King Jr. and Robert McNamara, to protest the growing violence in his country. Throughout all of his work, his teaching consistently emphasized "engaged Buddhism," stressing the importance of community, understanding, and mindfulness.[3]

Thich Nhat Hanh's willingness to speak truth in the face of incredible opposition is a testament to his great courage and commitment to nonviolent action in the world. An "engaged Buddhist" doesn't just apply the principles of Buddhism to solving the problems within the self, but also seeks to apply them to the problems of the world.[4] For the engaged Buddhist, there is no separation between contemplation and action, and indeed there is no intrinsic separation between self and community. Many make the mistake of assuming that meditation is a passive act. However, even though the body is usually still in meditation, the mind of the student is very much alive. Translating this inner activity to outer engagement has been a major part of Thich Nhat Hanh's life's work.

Today, Thich Nhat Hanh is demonstrating the possibilities of this alternative approach to learning through a new movement, called Wake Up Schools. The schools in this network make a commitment to incorporating mindfulness into the course of the day. Thich Nhat Hanh seeks to cultivate mindfulness in education through retreats and lectures for educators as part of the Wake Up Schools program.[5] Using Plum Village, Thich Nhat Hanh's monastery in France, as a base, the Wake Up Schools movement creates a space for sustainable and lasting happiness in children through pedagogy that nurtures not just the mind but also the heart of the student.[6] This approach represents a powerful counternarrative to the accountability-driven reforms currently being implemented in the United

States. By shifting away from standardization and the homogenization of learning, Thich Nhat Hanh offers a fresh outlook on what is possible for students and teachers alike.

THE WHOLE PERSON

The foundation of Merton's perspective on education was "the formation of the whole person." Merton believed that teachers can facilitate a fuller understanding of the whole self through the teaching of the whole person and the application of contemplative methods like journaling, silence, and meditation. In his work *Love and Living*, Merton describes the basic purpose of education as showing "a person how to define himself authentically and spontaneously in relation to his world."[7] Thus a valuable education is one that helps the student explore the self and strip away all the layers of inauthenticity.

The only way to do this, in Merton's view, is through contemplation. Silence and solitude offer the direct experience necessary to truly encounter the authentic self. By turning inward, we gain unfettered access to our selves. Merton critiqued the modern educational focus on the mind alone. If the mind is a place of duality, where our thoughts seek to sort experiences into distinct categories of good and bad or right and wrong, for Merton the heart is a place of unity, where multiple feelings, beliefs, and experiences can coexist simultaneously. In order to awaken the eyes of the heart and one's intuition, education has to foster a more unified experience of both the inner and outer worlds. Through this holistic approach, students can authentically engage in a lived experience, rather than just read from a textbook.

THE COMMON CORE AND THE CONTEMPLATIVE CORE

The Common Core now dominates the national conversation about education. This reform effort is attempting to increase consistency across the entire K-12 curriculum, as well as to raise standards of rigor and learning. While this may seem like a much-needed reform, the manner in which these changes have been implemented and the wave of high-stakes testing that has followed have only increased levels of anxiety and stress among students and teachers. What follows here is both a response to the Common Core and an outline of core principles at the heart of a contemplative perspective, the Contemplative Core.

The Contemplative Core

- **Slow down the classroom.** Move away from the notion that more content is better, and instead create time for students to make meaningful connections between the material they are studying and their lived experiences in the world.
- **Provide more opportunities in the day for silence and solitude.** Whether it's a simple reading at the start of the class or sitting in quiet meditation at the end, periods of stillness and silence develop healthy young people.
- **Consider placing the concept of service at the center of the classroom.** When students are encouraged to move beyond traditional notions of community service and volunteering so that they may more emphatically consider their place in the world, the experience is transformative. Creating moments for deep reflection allows students not

only to identify their gifts but also to think about how they might make an offering of those talents to meet a need in the world.

- **Make listening an active practice.** Compassionate and engaged listening is not a passive exercise. Teaching students how to better listen to others while also modeling it, as their teacher, can eventually create the practice by which students can better listen to themselves. Silence creates the tool, and listening is the practice.

- **Meditate.** There will be no significant change in the world of education until we learn and teach students to reconnect with and honor the present moment, whether we do this by just having them silently journal on a single prompt or by actually having them sit in the classroom and quietly observe their breath.

CONCLUSION

Unfortunately, much of the work and structure of schools today only contribute to the compartmentalization of students' lives. Their days are divided into subjects, arts, sports, and playdates. There is little to no space for reflection or for the interior life. The consequence of this division is a life that is fragmented, un-whole, and emotionally repressed. Authentic teaching, in contrast, is an act that engages and enacts the whole being, not just an aspect of the self. We can learn much from both Eastern and Western monastic traditions, in which silence and stillness create the inner space needed for the integration of the whole person.

MEDITATION ON SILENCE

This meditation can be both the easiest to lead and also the most unsettling if you or your class aren't used to long periods of quiet and stillness. I recommend starting this meditation with just a single minute, or even ten breaths, for a few sessions before stretching it across five- or ten-minute periods. This meditation can be done in a circle or with students seated behind their desks. If you intend to use this as an introductory meditation, with others following later, I strongly recommend meditating in a circle and establishing a consistent routine for the students.

Make sure the students are comfortable. Have them make any adjustments they might need, rotating their shoulders, relaxing their arms, and letting their legs be loose.

When they are ready, have them take three breaths and begin.

Invite the students to close their eyes and turn their gaze inward.

Invite them to follow their breath and take two more long breaths together.

With each breath, invite the students to settle into their seats and their breathing.

Remind them that although thoughts may pass through their minds, they should keep returning their focus back to their breath.

With each breath invite the students to move

deeper into themselves, turning their attention inward, away from the outside world.

Once you feel that a space and an inward commitment are established, explain to the students that you now invite them to count the next ten breaths themselves, silently.

At the end of those ten breaths, invite them to sit in silence for ten more breaths.

Lastly invite the students to continue to breathe as the whole class sits in silence.

At the end of whatever period you feel is appropriate for your class, slowly invite them back into the room. Encourage them to feel their feet on the ground again, maybe even have them wiggle their toes and fingers. Finally, but only when they are ready, invite them to take three long breaths and open their eyes.

CHAPTER FIVE

⤳⤳⤳

THE CLASSROOM

S tory is a beautiful way to weave our lives together, and it's a powerful tool in the classroom for connecting yourself to the students, as well as connecting the students to the curriculum. I use the archetypal elements of stories to create vivid guided meditations that lead through streams, mountains, and other worlds, and I also use story to encourage students to share their reflections. Creating a narrative and helping students feel like authors of their own lives is a key part of this experience. If the meditation can be experienced as a story, students can remember that life also has that same possibility. They are not simply living out someone else's wishes or desires; they have the creative power to construct their own dreams, whether in the inner worlds of their mind or the outer worlds of what they say and do.

But story is just one of the elements I draw upon in my classroom meditations. It serves to build a sense of community and shared experience, but other aspects of introducing meditation like building routines, supporting the exploration of interior space, and the use of questions as a guiding tool are also valuable to this process. It is the convergence of all these pieces that creates a healthy and powerful experience for students that can deepen their connection to self, one another, and the curriculum.

AN INVITATION

While there are many types of meditation, much of the meditation I've worked with draws heavily on the motifs of storytelling and visualization. Students look for a tangible experience, and I've learned that they will not return to something if they don't see or feel an immediate benefit. They are incredibly demanding and discerning consumers. I have also found over the years that ending meditations with strong components of imagery that draw from archetypal stories is very powerful. Whether the image is a doorway, a path, a dark forest, a mountaintop, or a cave, these simple cues bring students' imagination to life, and they often take the stories from a meditation far beyond the classroom walls.

Joseph Campbell spoke extensively about the power of the journey, the archetype of the hero in myth and literature, and the stages along the way as one becomes more fully human.[1] Yet in our obsession with fact and evidence we've lost sight of the deeper truths and lessons, both in these old tales and in the adventures that fill our lives. The very nature of the school year, with its renewing cycle of seasons, speaks of the Hero's Journey. The fall is marked by renewal, the winter by effort and toil, the spring by life, and the summer by full bloom. Along the way we meet challenges, teachers, friends, foes, gods, and goddesses, but most of all we meet ourselves.

The Hero's Journey lays out a common set of benchmarks found in almost all stories: the call, the refusal, the thresholds, the adventure, and the return, to name just a few. These benchmarks together form the narrative arc of the story. Similarly, each meditation also has a similar arc, as the list below reveals. It begins with a simple breathing period. It then moves into an invitation into the body. At this point the students cross an invisible threshold from their minds into their hearts. Meditation often explores personal challenges, unexpected aids, and the ultimate reward, self-discovery. The student is changed by the experience, only to return back to the classroom to share their insight and wisdom with others.

THE STAGES OF A GUIDED MEDITATION

1. **The Call.** The opening portion of the meditation is the Call. Think about how these first few breaths and moments invite the student into their bodies and out of their heads.

2. **The Threshold.** It is here in the second stage of the meditation that students either turn their attention to their mind's eye or drop their awareness into their heart. This motif is intended to move students into a deeper connection with themselves. Sometimes this is enough. In many meditations, particularly shorter ones, you can comfortably stop here and feel satisfied.

3. **The Journey.** If you want to move the meditation deeper, the next step is to invite the students to begin

the journey. This is where you might introduce the idea of a road, a path, or even a doorway. Before exploring this next phase, I often invite students to look at the stones on the road, maybe observe what grows along the path. It is very important here to bring them into contact with the path or help them visualize it intimately before walking it.

4. **The Challenge.** Having students write down the challenge, or their questions for the meditation, *before* starting the meditation is a powerful way to create the circumstances of the challenge. The questions might be personal or topical.

Questions about Self

- Why am I feeling this way?
- Is there anything challenging my growth as a student and an individual?
- What is blocking me from achieving my goals?

Questions about a Topic

- Is there anything I should know about my topic that I don't?
- What questions still remain unanswered?
- Where should I look to find new insights or overlooked information?

5. **The Return.** Here at the end of the meditation, students have the opportunity to process and then share their experiences with their peers. After taking this journey or engaging in the meditation,

what would they like to share and in what ways do they feel different than before the meditation?

LESSONS FROM MY FIRST GUIDED MEDITATION

I ran my first guided classroom meditation in 2012. I had led meditations before and I'd been part of a Meditation Club, but I'd never tried meditating in a classroom setting. However, given the auspicious date and all the rumors flying around concerning the Mayan calendar and the end of the world, I decided to use one of the days before the December break to lead a visual meditation on time.

This was a huge leap of faith for me on so many levels. First, up to that point all of the meditations I'd led in Meditation Club were very short and only skimmed the surface. Second, I had rarely if ever closed my eyes while guiding a meditation or even risked the possibility of students having a deeper experience, outside of my control. And third, I simply didn't know what to say or even where to begin.

As I look back at that first meditation, I now realize that two things served me well in taking such a great risk. First, there was a larger global conversation around the Mayan calendar and 2012. This helped place students in a mindset that facilitated a natural interest in and curiosity about the topic, also possibly encouraging other conversations and experiences that strayed from the mainstream. Second, I was engaging in this meditation just before the school break.

Most teachers know that the week before a school break, and especially the last couple of days of that week, are usually low on productivity. In many classrooms students might watch movies or play games, but in general school takes on a celebratory tone, especially before the December break. This proved to be a perfect opportunity to introduce a meditation into the classroom. It tapped into that desire to do something different, but it also fostered a series of desirable outcomes, more than what would have been achieved by just showing the students another movie.

The other advantage of introducing that first meditation in December was that it gave me time. I was dealing with a class of students who were new to the experience, and starting in December had given me over three months to establish my classroom norms and expectations before sitting in a circle with the twenty-five of them and closing my eyes. I would never encourage someone to engage in meditation before the basic norms and expectations of the class were well established.

I now realize that my first guided meditation left me with two gems to pass along to you. First, use what is going on in the world or in your curriculum to engage your students and lead them into a deeper conversation. And second, do not engage in meditation before the basic norms and expectations of the class are well established. The setting and timing of a first meditation loom large in shaping student experience and building the framework for success, not just in that moment but also in future meditation experiences.

ROUTINES

Routine is highly contextual; whatever works best for you is what works best for you. All my guidelines are just suggestions. I do recommend that whatever routine you establish, you stick with it as much as possible. Here is a simple list of things you might ask the students to do before starting a meditation in your class.

1. Arrange your chairs in a circle.
2. Find a seat. (In Meditation Club I also include a stretch after students find their seats.)
3. Place your notebook and pencil under your chair.
4. Get comfortable, sit up straight, and square your feet to the ground.
5. Close your eyes, take three breaths, and begin.

The meditation proceeds from there.

Lastly, after the meditation is over, have students take a moment to write in their notebook. Then invite them to share with others in the class. You can give them a specific prompt to reflect on or just let them write whatever comes to mind.

STUDENT REFLECTION ON A GUIDED MEDITATION

To be honest, I don't remember exactly what took place over the fifteen minutes of that first classroom meditation back in 2012, but I do know that the interest in and desire for more were almost instant. What follows are short but poignant examples of how a simple guided meditation can put a student in touch with a topic in ways one could never imagine. Once the mind is opened, the possibilities are endless.

The meditation in question took place after students had completed a project that asked them to identify an object from one of the civilizations studied in the class. There was a great deal of freedom in student selection, as they were allowed to pick their own object. In the end they were asked to include both a short description of the object, like one might find in a museum, and a three-dimensional re-creation of it. Students wrote the following paragraphs as they reflected both on the final project and also on the meditations that guided them to a closer connection with their object.

> For this last meditation, I found myself again at Stonehenge with a Druid. I think the reason I continue to be drawn to Stonehenge is because of the energy and lore surrounding it. At Stonehenge, it was in modern day [times], and the Druid and I were surrounded by tourists but they could not see us. I think this demonstrated how long Stonehenge has been around, and how many people and events it has seen over these 10,000 years. The gift of gratitude I gave the Druid was a sextant, because they had such great astrological understanding and I wanted to add to their knowledge of the cosmos. When I handed him the sextant in the middle of Stonehenge, I saw a look of understanding in his eyes, as I had uncovered some of the many secrets about the Druids through tangible research and previous meditations throughout the research process. When we came back through the doorway, I felt a sense of closure, but also many new questions flooded my mind — one being how did they know so much about the stars above and the earth below?
>
> Kevin Hendrick
> April 23, 2015

As Kevin noted in his reflection, he had engaged in several meditations on this topic before this one. What is amazing is the depth and the connection that he felt with a topic almost ten thousand years old. Repeated meditations on the same topic have a capacity for deepening the experience and learning in profound ways. Here is another example from a student who finished a lengthy project on Glastonbury Abbey before engaging in a final meditation:

> I found myself in a place where I have always been truly happy, the shrine at camp in the foothills of Colorado. Gazing out over the lands beyond, I looked forward and saw the foothills give way to plains; I saw the lights of Denver. Turning around, I found myself gazing at the treacherous Rocky Mountains, imagining myself atop them. I was alone; I was at peace.
>
> Another door began to formulate before me, and as I stepped toward it, I realized it was different than before. It was heavy, oak, like the gates to a castle. It creaked loudly as it opened; it had not been used in some time. It was dark inside as I stepped in. I was in an unfamiliar place and I did not recognize my darkened surroundings. However, I knew why I was there, and I knew what I needed to do.
>
> Now calm, I rushed to Galahad in his seat, and offered him my gift that was bestowed unto me. He took it, and drank it, and his soul was purified. I felt the scene start to fold into itself, and I soon found myself back at my camp, and in time, back at the beach. I opened my eyes and felt finally truly connected with my research topic.
>
> Daniel Bettino
> April 21, 2015

Where did these images, words, and thoughts come from? I don't know. What I do know is that the depth and creativity of student reflections has remained consistent over the years, and these creations have never ceased to amaze me. Students need to learn how to reconnect with their inner lives, and also with the curriculum, in deeply personal ways. There will be no significant change in the world of education if the content we teach remains a static, impersonal object.

VISUALIZATION MEDITATION: THE POWER OF STORY

Stories are incredibly powerful ways to connect to one another. They are a part of our DNA as the way we teach meaning and value to our students. The moment a teacher says, "Once upon a time," immediately everyone in the class will lift their heads up and listen — story is so much a part of the fabric of our being.

Educational scholar Parker Palmer writes about teaching as a process of "creating a space."[2] By this he means that teaching is more than just creating a physical space in the classroom for questions and discussion; it's also the process by which a space is created in the mind of each learner for self-discovery and reflection. In this process of reflection, students grow beyond their limited notions of themselves and discover an even deeper well of self-awareness and compassion for those around them. Stories often offer the entry points into these interior spaces.

Education at its finest awakens students to their authorship and the power of their voices, an awakening of their talent for creating and telling their own stories. In kindergarten we engage in the simple but powerful activity of "Show and Tell." In many ways, this is an act of storytelling — it's an opportunity for each child to share something about themselves and also for students to learn something about each other. As students get older we reduce the time for storytelling; we ask fewer questions about our students' lives and share even less about our own. However, a simple, well-intentioned story in the middle of a lesson or a visualization meditation, built along the principles of the ancient stories, is an invitation back into the world, the self, and learning.

I engage in content-based meditations only three times a year. This type of meditation draws heavily from the motifs of story and of journeys. It is very exhausting and requires routines. This might seem like an overblown warning, but I cannot impress upon you enough the fact that this type of meditation should not be engaged in without preparation. Do not attempt content-based meditation lightly or on the spur of the moment. However, if you do the legwork ahead of time, you'll be amazed by what comes out of it. This process has the potential to help students engage aspects of their mind and consciousness that they might not otherwise use in the course of the school day. (This exercise is especially valuable given the number of low-order skills we tend to focus on in schools today.)

Please note that content-based meditation also has the potential to tap into pain, trauma, or memories that students would otherwise not wish to think about. There are many feelings and emotions that reside just beneath the surface of our students' mental lives. When you invite one to leave their head and enter the heart, the water can become deep fairly quickly. And in many cases it is only after accessing or discovering some such dormant emotional wounding that the wound is able to be properly healed with the help of other, more suitable professionals in the school, including guidance counselors, psychologists, and a student's family.

Meditation doesn't create something that isn't there, but it often will bring to the surface what has been hidden away. I believe it is far more beneficial for adults and professionals to be there to support students in working through these challenges than avoiding them and leaving students to their own devices to figure out a way to cope. The positive potential of a well-supported and well-timed meditation is much greater than the negative, and in my opinion, it is well worth the risk. Avoiding the emotional lives of our students and pretending that emotions don't shape their academic worlds is a naïve approach to the classroom. Often it is through their emotional connection to a topic, or subject, or teacher that students thrive as young scholars.

I've come to believe that we use only about 10 percent of our potential. Meditation offers a path back into that potential and to the capacity that has been lost. What is amazing and surprising is the depth and richness of the unexplored regions of the mind and subconscious, as well as what resides there. Having worked with both adults and children, I also have to say that kids and teenagers have an easier time accessing these aspects of the self. For them, all the extra programming and the narrow views of identity that we adults have don't exist yet, or aren't as firmly formed.

In kids and young people there still remains a sense of wonder and openness that many adults have lost. However, that wonder and openness are already being diminished even over the course of a student's high school years. I can see a difference between ninth and twelfth graders in the ability to use meditation as a tool for self-discovery. The window for risk taking and identity exploration starts to close during these formative years, and it closes fast. Students begin to internalize false identities around external successes and feedback. And while these identities do have value, they become problematic when they come at the expense of other, more authentic identities and potential for growth.

Before I start a guided meditation I link the experience to something I'm doing in the curriculum. This is always valuable, but particularly so in content-based meditation. The more the meditation can be tied to academic work, the better. As a history teacher, I tie this type of meditation to an assignment and more specifically to the research and writing processes. I find these meditations to be a perfect complement to an otherwise heady experience. After the assignment is given, I wait two or three weeks before initiating the first meditation, then I offer the second meditation before the writing process begins (about two-thirds of the way through the assignment), and finally we end with a meditation at the end, to close the whole experience. All three meditations are set up the same way, but all three leave an enormous amount of space for students' unique experiences and interests.

1. The first meditation is an introduction to the topic.
2. The second is an exploration of the driving questions.
3. The third meditation is a reflection.

The Three Questions of the Content-Based Meditation

The three sessions of the content-based meditation all take on a similar form. After students have created a circle with their chairs, and before we start the meditation, I have students write down three questions in their notebooks. The questions must relate directly to their research topics and address aspects of their subject that still remain unknown. I always encourage students to ask questions that might not be simply answered through primary or secondary sources. I encourage them to ask questions of individuals, personal questions whose answers may have been lost in the pages of history. I also suggest that their final question be open-ended. This question might include an aspect of their topic that they simply hadn't considered. "Is there anything I am missing or overlooking in my research?" The question doesn't need to be written down, but it does need to venture into an unexplored territory of their research.

Once the students have written down these three questions, I tell them to place their notebooks and pencils beneath their chairs and prepare to have their questions answered. The next few minutes of the meditation are almost identical to the opening of any meditation I lead. I make sure that students have a good physical posture on their chair and that everyone is in their own space, and then I begin. I always start with our three opening breaths. I encourage the students to close their eyes, turn their gaze inward, and then I lead them in a short body scan to bring them out of their heads and into their bodies.

I then have the students imagine a place that feels very safe and comforting to them. This space can be inside or outside; it doesn't matter. When the students find that space in their mind, I then invite them to explore it. What do they see? What do they feel? What do they smell? I also ask them if they see anyone else in the space, and if so, to disinvite that person at least for the next few minutes. Once they are alone, I ask the students to look around again, this time making a complete 360-degree scan of the space.

As they come back to facing forward in their minds, I tell them to imagine that a closed door now stands in front of them, maybe five or ten feet away. If they are out in nature, the door could stand upright, as if supported by some unforeseen force. If they are inside, the door could be part of the existing space, or something entirely new. How the door is situated doesn't matter. What does matter is that the door and what resides behind it are connected to their topic. I then ask them to approach the closed door and begin to see and feel its power. I ask them to look closely at the door and notice all the intricate details. What is it made of? How big is it? What does the knob or handle look like? The more detailed and specific this part is, the better it will be for the next portion of the meditation, which is driven by observation.

When the students are ready, I ask them to reach out to grip the handle. I tell them that this door is connected to their past *and* to their topic. "In a moment," I say, "we are going to open the door and take three breaths." I explain that when they reach the third breath they will find themselves on the other side of the door and in a new time and space. After this setup I encourage them to step forward and open the door. As they open it, they take three breaths and step across the threshold. As they continue through the breaths, they feel themselves moving through a vast space, as if they are taking the biggest step of their whole lives. When they reach the third breath, the students suddenly feel their feet hit solid ground.

Once they "land" in this new space, I immediately guide them to look at their feet. What is below them? Slowly, I then guide them in looking at their ankles, their wrists, their clothes, even their hair. Then I ask them to consider where they might be. Is it night, or day? Is it sunny, or cloudy? I then ask them to recall their first question.

I take the students through this process with all three questions. Then, when they are done, they take three more breaths. As the first three breaths brought them to this new place, the last three breaths bring them out of it. The first breath takes them back to the door; the second, back to the heart space; and the third, back to the classroom. Before the students open their eyes, I ask them to connect with their feet again, to feel them on the floor. I have found this meditation to be a dizzying experience, so returning to their feet is a tool to pull them into the present. It helps ground them.

As soon as the students open their eyes, I have them immediately turn to their notebooks and write or draw what they experienced. I remind them not to overthink their responses, just to get them on paper. Like a dream, these images and thoughts evaporate quickly, so it is advised to let the students write them down before they speak.

Tips for Guiding a Visual Meditation

- Draw on images students know from the content of the class.
- Build the images gradually, from familiar to extraordinary.
- Draw upon nature as a powerful tool for moving them deeper into the visualization.
- Doorways can mark thresholds, and so can labyrinths or mazes.
- Keep it broad so students can use their intuitive mind to call up whatever images they desire.
- Go slowly. Students need time to process imagery in visualizations. The subconscious often speaks in a language that is cryptic and symbolic.
- You have to convince students that there is no right or wrong way of doing this. The more open and supportive you can be, the better.

- Lastly, keep inviting the students to return their attention to their feet throughout the meditation. Wherever they are, have them feel their feet on the ground. This will help center the experience from start to finish.

CONCLUSION

When guiding a meditation, let go of what you hope those you lead will experience; let go of your own expectations. You might have a specific objective in mind, or want those you lead to come away with a certain learning outcome, but this is secondary to what they create or connect to in their minds. Letting go can be incredibly challenging, as so much of our work as educators is defined by control and measured by outcomes.

I also find that meditation is most effective when the narration is framed as an invitation. This allows students to imagine as freely and deeply as they would like and feel most comfortable with, without worrying about being right or wrong. For example, I love to use the image of the labyrinth as an entry point into guided meditations that have a strong visual component. You should feel free to use whatever image is most comfortable for you; that comfort will certainly be transferred to your students. Some might find it more useful to use a specific image from nature, maybe the beach or the mountains; others might find more comfort in an image from home, like a bedroom or fireplace. It doesn't matter; the feeling is more important than the actual imagery. When presented with the invitation and given the inspiration, the students will do the rest.

THE STAIRCASE MEDITATION

Find a comfortable position on a chair or cushion. Place a lit candle three or four feet in front of you, and lower your gaze or close your eyes. Take three breaths and begin.

With each breath, simply watch as the air moves in and out.

Follow your breath into your lungs, your arms, and your heart center.

Scan your body as you take this next inhale.

Follow your breath through your lungs, into your stomach, your hips, your legs, and all the way to the bottom of your feet, and then back up again until you reach the top of your head. As you follow these next few breaths, just let them move through your whole body without judgment, without restraint, without fear.

Notice any blocks in your body as you continue the meditation, any places where you are storing or holding on to unwanted emotions from the past.

When you find these places, just breathe into them without force of thought or desire of outcome and imagine the blocks dissolving.

On this next inhale, move back into your heart center.

Imagine a light here, and give that light a color.

As you take this next inhale, imagine this light expanding, like a balloon filling with air.

Let this color move into your heart, your lungs, your chest, until it surrounds your whole body.

As this light expands, imagine it surrounding you and permeating your whole being.

On this next inhale, move into your mind's eye.

Before you is a staircase. This is a magical staircase that represents your life, the path you have taken to this point.

I invite you to step onto the stairs. No judgment, just observing and noticing.

Begin to notice that on each step is a moment from your life.

Walk up or down these stairs as you move through your life, pausing every few steps, every few years.

As you get toward the end, step off this staircase for a moment and imagine yourself as a little being, just one or two years old. What do you see? A toy? A friend? A stuffed animal?

After you have made that connection, step back onto the staircase.

Now a doorway is in front of you. Take a moment to look at this doorway. What is it made of? How does it feel? How does it open?

When you are ready, open this doorway and step into the space.

This is an immense space. It is a space you have known before, a space you have always known.

As you look out, imagine you can see your whole life in front of you — all the people, all the paths, all the adventures you have known. For a moment just pause in this light and radiance.

As you look down at your feet, notice a book. This

is a book of your life. Let your heart-radiance illuminate this book. In the book you can see all the gifts and lessons you have carried across this and all your lives.

Let this book reawaken all the aspects of yourself you have forgotten. Let this book reawaken your past, and your future.

When you are ready, please close the book.

Look one more time around you and see the beautiful light that permeates the entire space.

It is a light connected to your heart.

Take a deep inhale and feel this light fill your heart.

And then, and only then, take three long breaths, focusing on the exhale, and when you reach the final one, open your eyes.

CHAPTER SIX

∽∽ ∽∽ ∽∽

MEDITATION CLUB

Bringing meditation into a school or building is a delicate and lengthy process. It requires the navigation of a number of constituents and interests. And if it is not done well initially, it can have a huge consequence for the long-term viability or success of a program.

In my experience, this type of work is most successfully integrated into the school when it is initiated by teachers or students, or even better — both. Teachers' grassroots desire to address the growing concerns and anxieties permeating the classroom environment, along with a motivation to integrate the work into their classrooms, is crucial to its success. The basis for all the work I have done in the school and district started with one small group, Meditation Club.

Our Meditation Club really began when Jak approached me about his science project, over seven years ago. He was an eleventh grader, and I'd known him since he took my class in ninth grade. As part of an independent study project for science class, he wanted to explore the benefits of meditation on the teenage mind. Jak had already done a lot of research on the topic and just needed to create an experiment to support his hypothesis. He also knew from our conversations both inside and outside the classroom that I studied and practiced meditation. He thought I'd be the perfect faculty advisor to join his experiment, and I'm eternally grateful he invited me to take part.

That first week there was just a small group of us, no more than five or six other students, including myself. We gathered in a circle in one of the science classrooms at the end of the lunch period, and Jak led us in a quiet meditation. The first meditation was primarily silent, with only a word or two from Jak guiding us in finding the right posture or gently reminding us to come back to our breaths. What I didn't know at the time, and struggle to believe even today, was that the circle Jak initially formed for his science experiment would eventually become an organization that would serve as the mindfulness bedrock of the whole school — Meditation Club. This chapter will explore the creation of this club and the ways in which it might be replicated in other schools.

OUR MEDITATION CLUB

Over the years, from the first week to the last week of school, the club has met continually every Wednesday. The size of our circle fluctuates throughout the year, from just two to sometimes over thirty meditators. Even if only one person shows up, the club still runs a meditation. The club is also open to any member of the school community, from faculty and students to secretaries and administrators. With the ebb and flow of the membership has come an evolution in how the club functions.

The club always gathers in the same classroom, and always during the lunch period. The meditation itself doesn't take place until the last twenty minutes of the period, and students are invited to sit, eat, and talk beforehand. As we get closer to the time of meditating, I usually give people a five-minute warning, and then they finish up their lunches and begin to move desks and gather the chairs into a circle. Meanwhile, I close the classroom door and put up a sign that reads "Quiet, Please. Meditation in Progress." I encourage students to turn their phones off, and then one of the club members begins the meditation with a simple stretch. The stretch, always student run, consists of some gentle standing backbends, a twist or two, and a stretch of our hands and arms, for all the texting and typing we do throughout the day. Once the stretch is completed, students find a seat in the circle and I join them.

As I mentioned before, I'm very intentional about where I sit, and I recommend you do the same. I almost always sit with my back to the door of the classroom. I think this serves several purposes, including holding the energy of the circle and positioning myself in a way that drowns out any noise from the hallway. I'm fortunate to have a classroom away from some of the busier passageways in the school, but as you can imagine, it sometimes gets noisy toward the end of the period if you meet during lunch. I'd recommend finding a quiet room or explaining the need for quiet to the students who routinely gather outside your door before their next class. While you never want to find yourself competing against outside noise, you want to do your best to be prepared for it.

Once I find my seat and check to make sure everyone in

the group has also found their seats, I gently encourage them to keep their feet about hip-distance apart and to try and space themselves out evenly, respecting the space of their neighbors. I've said this before and feel it is worth emphasizing again: particularly with kids, clearing personal space and defining boundaries are ingredients to making meditators feel safe and comfortable enough to turn their attention inward. I also might encourage them to make any last-minute adjustments and take a final twist or two to help with the alignment of their spine. I then instruct them to place their hands in a comfortable position, either on their thighs or palm in palm. And then with three breaths, we begin.

Looking back over the last seven years, I am amazed at the number of club members, and in particular club presidents, who have gone on to attend many of the top universities in the country. I don't believe this is a coincidence, as the capacity to reflect and to nurture our inner lives enriches the learning process and deepens all our experience. And don't take my word for it. Here is a reflection from the original founder of the club, Jak Maguad, who recently graduated from Harvard. Jak describes his motives for creating this organization and how it changed over the years. He also does a wonderful job identifying the benefits and challenges of meditation in schools, particularly for young people.

> In my opinion, the hardest part about introducing people to meditation is getting them started — people tend to shy away from it if they don't understand it or if they try it and do it incorrectly. It's easy to get discouraged if you try it and have to struggle on your own. I think that in a school setting, it's possible to leverage a lot of

things that make this introduction easier: meditating in a group can make it less intimidating, especially with other beginners, and guided meditations from more experienced friends or teachers can also be great for supporting people who are new to it. I found that convincing people to start was the hard part, because once they understood how it could help them and knew how to meditate correctly, they were much more enthusiastic. I also think that a huge reason our Meditation Club took off had to do with the social aspect and the sense of community that we built, which was also made more powerful by a school setting. I remember that when we were growing very quickly, a lot of our new members often heard about us through word of mouth or were brought to us directly by a friend.

Jak Maguad

2018

EVOLUTION OF MEDITATIONS

When Jak first began Meditation Club, the meditations were primarily silent and lasted eight to twelve minutes. Today the meditations have grown in length and explore a variety of images and topics. Some of those images have been inspired by the calendar, others by a conversation we'd had only minutes before, and some by a simple request. The source of the inspiration is secondary; what matters most is the leader's presence and ability to authentically lead the students out of the everyday buzz of their minds and into a quieter space of reflection.

I almost always begin these meditations with a focus on the breath. Sometimes I'll have the meditators practice alternate nostril breathing, and other times I'll have them place their hand over their heart, feeling their chest rise and fall. In the vast majority of cases, I simply have the students become aware of their breath by breathing in through their nose and out through their mouth. Even if students do this for only three or four breaths, the simple act has the powerful effect of drawing their attention away from all the things buzzing around in their head and calming their mind.

From this opening strategy, I usually invite students to become more aware of their expanding breath, noticing when it first begins and becoming aware of the point where it ends. With each breath, and in each direction, I encourage students to allow their thoughts to quiet and to return to the breath when they find themselves getting distracted. As the meditation deepens, this rhythmic breathing can also be the soundtrack behind the leader's voice that draws students into themselves.

From the breath focus, I often move into a scan of the whole body, inviting the students to inhale into each area of the body, one by one, and using the exhale to clear and open blocked areas. This simple yet powerful tool can be used on a physical, an energetic, and even an emotional level, inviting students to visualize each area of stickiness or stress in the body, starting with the head and moving all the way down to the feet.

Knowingly or unknowingly, we often hold emotions and even trauma within our bodies on a cellular level. While a simple body scan might not be enough to clear deep-seated feelings or emotions, facilitators must be aware of the potential this practice can have to awaken old, sometimes forgotten, memories. At the end of the body scan, it is really worth emphasizing and detailing the exploration of the feet. Inviting students to take an extra minute to feel their feet on the floor or imagine roots growing out from the bottoms of their toes can help ground and center them for the day.

If you are new to leading meditations, I would stop after the body scan and regrounding. However, when you feel comfortable enough and ready to move forward, you can continue, leading the students deeper into a visual meditation. Drawing upon images and unconscious symbols can be a powerful way for students to explore an issue, a challenge, a goal, a relationship, or an aspect of self in their lives.

For example, when exploring the heart, I might use the image of a flower; for the breath, the image of the ocean or waves on the shore. For issues of rooting or centering, I might explore a tree or a forest. For thoughts moving across the mind, I might play with the images of the sky and clouds. There is really no right or wrong metaphor here — the idea is to connect students with images and symbols that they can relate to, that are nonthreatening and comforting. Simple images of the summer or a grandparent's home can be comforting, while the mention of homework or tests can instantly trigger anxiety. As you experiment with images and words, you'll find you are almost like a conductor, tapping into the musical landscape of the interior.

At the end of every meditation, it is worth making time for each student to share their experience from the meditation. What did they feel? What did they see? How did it compare to earlier meditations? Students often will revisit the same places over multiple meditations, and these places shift in subtle yet meaningful ways. With a simple glance or gentle nod of encouragement, give space to those who are willing to share their experience. Not only will this prove invaluable in guiding your future meditations, providing you with feedback and insight on what worked and what didn't work, but it will also help foster a sense of community among the members.

MEDITATION CLUB RULES

Over the years as our Meditation Club has grown, we have tried to keep the rules and guidelines simple:

1. All are welcome.
2. All are respected.
3. All are honored.

Along with these rules I have outlined below a simple set of recommendations to assist anyone who might be interested in creating a similar organization at their school.

MEDITATION CLUB GUIDELINES

Let students take the lead. If you can get a core group of students to spearhead the initial recruitment effort, this can be empowering for both them and the club. A lot of your members will probably come to their first session having heard about it from another member. Later in the year you might ask students to run the opening stretch or even the meditation itself. I always ask students ahead of time so they aren't put on the spot. Generally speaking, the more students can be involved in leadership, the more successful the club will be.

Keep it simple. One benefit of the club is its consistency. Trying to run elaborate meditations or lengthy visualizations every week is too much. Yes, maybe you will have a special meditation around the solstice or the end of the year, but in general stick to the same simple routine. I have found that offering a simple ten-minute meditation at the end of lunch on Wednesdays works really well. If you have multiple lunch periods, maybe offer a meditation before school. The trick is to avoid times that are so complicated you or the students struggle to make sense of when the next meeting is.

Run it. From the first Wednesday of school in September to the last Wednesday in June, we always run a meditation, even if only one other person shows up. The numbers will fluctuate throughout the year, but I always run a meditation, no matter how many people are present. If no one shows up, don't cancel. You never know how a meditation might add to the positive energy of the space and the school. Use the time to nurture your own practice.

All are welcome. There should be no restrictions on joining the meditations. Students might come one time and not return for three months; it doesn't matter. I also welcome everyone in the school: students, faculty, and even administrators. Classroom aides and secretaries have joined our meditations, and on the rare occasion, alumni will even return.

All are respected. Regardless of our beliefs, our opinions, or our backgrounds, all of which shape the meditation experience, respect for all participants is crucial to creating an inclusive environment. As the advisor, it is paramount that you play a role in cultivating this safe space through your own actions and words, being careful to avoid tying the practice specifically to one belief system or set of political ideologies.

All are honored. I always make time for people to share at the end of the meditation. Even a simple meditation can awaken feelings, thoughts, and emotions that need to be voiced. I don't mind asking my next class to wait outside the door if it allows a student to share their experience for an extra minute or two. Nothing is more valuable than giving students space to share their reflections and feel heard.

Passing the torch. As the club grows, it is exciting and empowering to have students lead the meditations. You can also be intentional about the subject of the meditations given what is happening around you. For example you might incorporate meditations around stress during exam time, meditations on nature in the spring, or meditations on loss after tragedy. Students will give you insight into the issues and emotions they are struggling with, but you have to ask them first. I often either ask a student to lead a meditation or I ask them what they'd like to focus on in the meditation before I start. I find this a very effective method to create meaningful experiences for everyone in the space.

CONCLUSION

As I reflect on the growth of our Meditation Club over the years, I think that much of its success and strength stem from its simplicity and consistency. The presence of the club each Wednesday has come to meet a variety of unexpected needs in the school, from aiding the community through tragedy to helping seniors find space for making decisions about college. In the end, the rules of the club are secondary. It is the presence and the space of regular meditation in the form of a club that matter most.

THE POND MEDITATION

Place a lit candle three or four feet in front of you. Find a comfortable position on a chair or cushion. Make any adjustments you might need, rotate your shoulders, relax your arms, and let your legs be loose. When you are ready either lower your eyes into a soft forward gaze or, if you are comfortable doing so, close your eyes. Take three breaths and begin.

Try to breathe in through the nose and out through the mouth. Make the breath deliberate. With each breath, begin to deepen your awareness. Close your eyes.

Lengthen the inhale.

Lengthen the exhale.

Feel everything beginning to relax. Your shoulders, your fingers, your toes.

As you breathe, set an intention of finding balance with your breath. For example, make the inhale as long as the exhale. Find that pause at the start of the breath, and find that pause at the end.

Let your thoughts wander, but always come back to the breath. As you notice your next thought, see it, feel it, and then release it.

Notice when the breath first enters your body, and notice when it last leaves your mouth.

Start to drop out of your mind and into your body.

On this next breath, feel the inhale in your neck and shoulders. Imagine it as a cooling liquid, softening and relaxing your whole body. Feel the breath in your biceps and triceps, your elbows and your wrist.

Feel it all the way down to your palms and your finger-tips. As you exhale, feel everything go.

Come back to your breath and to the center of your body.

Feel yourself dropping even deeper into your heart, beating in your chest. Imagine you can see pre-cisely how your heart sends energy out to your whole body.

Imagine you can soften and lighten your heart with your next breath. Breathe into that space, and feel your heart open.

Now drop even deeper into your body, beneath your heart, your core, your hips. Feel yourself drop all the way down into your shins, your ankles, and your feet.

As you breathe in, feel the back of your feet, the inside and the outside of your feet.

Take another deep breath and feel your toes. With each breath, soften and relax your feet.

As you take this next breath, picture yourself standing at the edge of a body of water, be it lake, pond, or ocean. Feel your feet on that shore. Imagine the surface of the water is a mirror of the surface of your mind. Is it smooth or rough? Calm or turbulent?

Each time you have a thought, imagine it falling into the water. Notice how some of your thoughts are big and some are small. Each thought sends a ripple across the water.

Think about the things you have to do today or the things you did yesterday. Even think about the things you will do tomorrow.

One by one release them, and one by one let them be absorbed by the water.

Now begin to imagine your mind soften and widen.

Imagine your mind is like the surface of that water. With each breath send out a wave of calming and relaxing energy until it becomes as still as a mirror.

Take this next breath and imagine your mind as wide as the sky above and as still as the water below.

Just for a moment, relax in that stillness. Let everything else dissolve away.

When you are ready, take another breath and come back to your body. Keep your eyes closed, and feel your fingers and your feet.

Take one more long exhale and gently open your eyes.

CHAPTER SEVEN

∽∽∽∽∽∽

HIGH SCHOOL

When I was fifteen I read a popular book that has since been reissued many times, *The Alchemist*.[1] This novel, written by Paulo Coelho, had a powerful effect on my adolescent mind. It presented life as a great mystery and adventure, full of omens, signs, and callings. This story invited me into a shift in the way I perceived the world, from a place of tasks and obligations to one of adventures and self-discovery. I went on to devour every book I could by Coelho. From top to bottom I read his collection, and I even started a correspondence with this illustrious author.

In the midst of my quest to learn more, another story resonated with me. This book was the first that Coelho had ever written, and one of only two that were semi-autobiographical in nature. This was the work that inspired him to write *The Alchemist* in the first place. *The Pilgrimage*, first published in 1987, detailed Coelho's journey along a medieval path that stretched from the French border with northwestern Spain to the magical land of Galicia and the city of Santiago.[2] So it was that as a teenager I vowed to walk the Camino de Santiago when I got older.

A dozen years later, after my second year in the classroom, the opportunity to fulfill this lifelong desire presented itself. My trip started a day after my sister's wedding. It would take me from Detroit to Paris to Madrid and finally land me in the Spanish city of Pamplona. What would unfold over the next thirty days and five hundred miles would profoundly alter my understanding of life and teaching.

The Camino was a journey of many unexpected twists and turns, unexpected friendships, and unexpected challenges, but more than anything it was a space for powerful reflection. My pilgrimage was characterized by long days of walking the dusty Spanish farm roads, and afternoons reflecting on larger questions of life and living. Essentially this experience solidified my professional desire to be a teacher, and it also shifted my understanding of the classroom as a space for adventures and nurturing student voices.

What I also learned from walking the Camino was the ability to connect to my breath and use it as a tool for coming into alignment with my body. In any activity, whether it's physically strenuous or just sitting, the breath is a calming force, offering constant feedback about both your physical state and your emotional capacity. Walking the Camino reinforced this connection and taught me how to use the breath to overcome what felt like insurmountable physical challenges. It also taught me how to share those insights with others.

The journey of any classroom, especially in high school, has many parallels to a pilgrimage. It opens with promise, is followed by struggle, and ends with the reward of reaching a destination, often very different from the one you initially set out to achieve. Learning from the grueling experiences of the Camino and using them to remind myself of the daily grind of teaching has served as a source of strength and inspiration in my work.

GETTING IN THE ZONE

It was late spring and one of the students in my class, who was also the captain of the lacrosse team, asked if I would lead the team in a meditation. Not wanting to overstep my bounds, I agreed, but only if the coach also gave the okay. I knew this was a great opportunity to expand the breadth and audience of the meditation work I was already doing. The coach gave his approval, and the team agreed to meet in my classroom thirty minutes before the start of their next playoff game. I asked that each player bring their lacrosse stick but leave the rest of their gear in the locker room.

The afternoon finally arrived, and one by one these young men walked into my room to find a circle of chairs. Some had black paint under their eyes and others had expressions of disinterest. While I recognized a few of the faces from class and a handful from Meditation Club, the vast majority had never meditated with me before, and I was fairly confident that many had never meditated, period. I skipped the usual stretch before the meditation and, sensing the tension that precedes high school playoff games, got right into it.

The breath is one of the most powerful tools in meditation; some say it is the cord that connects the mind and the body. It is a tool that I almost always emphasize at the start of any meditation, and I think is particularly crucial when dealing with athletes, who tend to be hyperaware of their breath. Using this to my advantage, I asked each of the players to close their eyes and find their breath. When students are anxious, as is the case before a big game or test, I encourage them to take three breaths through their nose. This has the effect of almost instantly calming their mind and nervous system.

Once I was confident that enough time had passed for each of the players to find their own breath and begin to regulate it to some degree, I then had everyone take three long inhales and exhales together. Honestly, if the team had done only this with me it probably would have been enough. Finding the breath and regulating it brought calm to their bodies, and the synchronicity of the breath across the room among all the players created a unity of focus and energetic link that gelled twenty-eight separate entities into one collective body.

Success in team sports depends on unity across all the players, dropping everyone into a state and place where communication occurs on a deeper and more intuitive level. This deeper level of play is often called "the zone." Meditation is a powerful tool for facilitating this type of play, bringing athletes out of their heads and into their centers, into their bodies. When they are able to align their centers with the center of the team, they become unstoppable. But when athletes begin to play from the mind, they begin to worry about the next move, and the game is lost.

Just a simple meditation on the breath can have this unifying impact, but in the case of the lacrosse team I wanted to take them even deeper. After facilitating this initial connection with the breath I then led the players in visualization. In this portion of the meditation, I guided them into a forest, with each player taking his own path into the woods, like in the Arthurian Grail legends. After they wandered through the forest, I encouraged them all to come together again in an opening, a meadow, where the circle of young men was re-formed and each player found his stick waiting in the center. I then had the players open their eyes and without a word head out to the field.

If you think I took this too far, you aren't alone. That whole night after the meditation I was nervously checking the internet to see if the score of the game was posted or if the coach had emailed me. Had I done too much with this visualization, should I just have stuck with the breathing exercise, should I have declined the opportunity to lead a meditation altogether? I finally fell asleep, still anxious that I'd created more of a distraction and overstepped my boundaries as a teacher.

The next morning, after a little breakfast and a cup of tea, I sat back down at the computer and refreshed my browser. The score suddenly popped up: 18 to 3. The team had won. I blinked again and read that the team opened with fifteen unanswered points. On one level, I couldn't believe what I was seeing. But it was an incredible affirmation of what I had observed, less dramatically, in myself and the students in Meditation Club. Meditation really can change things.

MEDITATION IN SCHOOL ASSEMBLIES

Since that pregame meditation, students and the student government have asked me, on more than one occasion, to lead a workshop or a school-wide meditation for their yearly half-day celebration. This celebration usually occurs right after midterms and marks a natural midpoint in the year. On these occasions I've led workshops on the chakras or meditations on goal setting. But once I led a school-wide meditation in the theater, accompanied by two musical guests who specialized in sound baths.

Taking that first deep breath and then closing my eyes to begin a large group meditation is always a leap of faith equivalent to jumping off the high board at the pool. But it was especially so in this case, as a group of 240 adolescents took the leap with me at the midyear assembly. With no rehearsal, the musician next to me began an exhilarating soundtrack to accompany the meditation. The ethereal notes were a bath of vibration and sound communicating a feeling and mood without words. After a few snickers and coughs, a quiet hush fell upon the whole room.

It's hard to underestimate the power of collective meditation. I've often seen a momentum build in a group that supports the process and depth in ways that are difficult to achieve alone. But I would warn anyone against leading such a large group of students in meditation until you are ready. I only agreed to this opportunity after several years of classroom practice. Use your own discernment to determine if you are ready for this next step. How comfortable are you in your ability to project your voice and hold the space for such a large audience? Also keep in mind that it takes a great deal of energy to hold that kind of space. Even the next day, I still felt drained from the experience.

There is an old saying: the teacher appears when the student is ready. Trust your students. There is a good chance that they will only ask you when they feel the whole school is ready for such an experience, and that you are ready to lead one.

The power and palatable energy of the room at the end of that school-wide meditation was something I'll never forget. A deep calm filled the space and settled upon the students. One guidance counselor told me afterward that she'd never heard the school so quiet. It was also amazing to see other teachers and administrators participating in the meditation. There wasn't a soul in the room with their eyes open. For a moment it felt like we were all one.

MEDITATION WORKSHOPS

Every year the parents ask me to lead a "Happiness Workshop" for graduating seniors during their last week of classes. I have to laugh because I've never billed myself as the "Happiness Teacher," and I'm sure some students in the first few weeks of class would strongly argue *against* such a title. Yet somehow students who practice meditation pick up on happiness as a by-product of this work and consider it the crux of the experience. Indeed, there are countless studies to support a link between meditation and happiness, and given the constant distractions and endless screen time filling students' days, turning inward does seem to cultivate a peace and sense of ease that foster happiness.

In the workshop, which I offer the graduating seniors, I rarely mention the word *happiness*, but rather I focus on gratitude, the doorway to happiness. I think Brother David Steindl-Rast, a Benedictine monk, said it best in his TED talk, "It is not happiness that makes us grateful. It's gratefulness that makes us happy."[3] In the workshop I also cover a short list of "dos and don'ts" for seniors as they head off to the next stage after graduation. Things like, "Do study abroad" and "Don't date your high school sweetheart." Most of the suggestions are tongue-in-cheek, but they open the space for the deeper work in a way that only humor can.

After my remarks and some small-group activities, I have students form a large circle in preparation for the meditation. The class is usually divided into two groups for the workshop, so each circle is between sixty and eighty students. This is really the maximum space my voice can fill without a microphone. Straining your voice or yelling is never conducive to creating a peaceful and calming environment. Practice in the space ahead of time.

After leading the students through several short breathing exercises and a body scan (you hopefully can see a common pattern to all the meditations by now), I have them turn their gaze inward. I always like to work in threes at this point in a meditation, and I often use a repetitive pattern to deepen the experience, repeating words and imagery. In this context I lead the students through a meditation that asks them to recall three individuals who helped them through their high school years. I lead them in a reflection on a family member, then a friend, and finally, an adult from school.

In recent years I have brought the students out of this meditation and immediately tasked them with writing a short thank-you note to one of those individuals. I then give them the chance to share that letter with the person if they happen to be in the room, and if not, I offer to deliver it personally. An outpouring of gratitude and a recognition of the impact we knowingly and unknowingly have on one another spread like wildfire through the room. Students are almost always in tears by the end, as they share and reflect on these moments. Meditation may be the path to the heart, but gratitude is what always opens the door.

CHAKRA WORKSHOPS AND LIFE DECISIONS

I have been fortunate enough to teach a workshop on the seven chakras, a concept from the Hindu belief system that envisions an energetic body as well as a physical one. The chakras are seven centers of energy in the body, starting at the base of the spine and working their way up to the top of the head. Each chakra has a color and quality to it.

My introduction to the chakras came many years after I began a personal practice of meditation, when I was invited to a chakra retreat. There we reviewed the Hindu belief system, and we learned about the colors and qualities of each of the chakras. I have taken that learning and knowledge and used it with students, letting it inform my instruction and my guided meditations, as well as my workshop on the seven chakras.

The first chakra, located at the base of the spine, is red, representing the root and one's connection to the earth. The second chakra, which is orange, is located below the navel, the emotional center of the body. This is a good place to explore in a body scan, as many emotions and dormant feelings are swallowed and kept within our stomachs. The next chakra is located in the solar plexus. This chakra is yellow and represents the will. Tapping into one's will or lack of will is a powerful way of seeing what is really driving one's life. Noticing another person's energy or other blocks in the will can be insightful as one considers major decisions.

The fourth chakra, and the bridge between the physical and spiritual plane, is the heart. The heart chakra is green. There are an infinite number of meditations that connect to the heart, and I would encourage anyone leading a meditation to draw upon this color as often as they like. Other symbols for the heart include candles, flowers, or any space that feels comfortable and welcoming.

A blue orb represents the fifth chakra, or the voice. This chakra reflects one's truth, or the ability to speak and live one's truth in the world. One could spend an entire year working with students on this idea. Helping kids both speak and act in accordance with their own truth is a very powerful lesson. A person can only live their truth if they have had the opportunity to sit with it, to explore their inner worlds and see what lies in their heart. This exploration corresponds well with the sixth chakra, which is located just above the brow and is often described as the third eye or the inner eye. The sixth chakra allows one to see into things; it is connected to insight and intuition. Many individuals struggle with a third eye that is blocked, either by one's self or by someone or something else. As you might have noticed, the voice, or fifth chakra, is located between the third eye and the heart. That offers a lesson because it is only when we see into things and speak from the heart that we can share words that are transformative — a powerful reminder for teachers as well as students.

The seventh and last chakra is located above the crown of the head. This chakra, represented by a purple halo, connects us to our highest selves. Having an open and balanced seventh chakra allows one to live a life not limited by personal or societal beliefs.

You may be wondering about the chakras' colors. I find that colors can be a very powerful visual tool for many students. Try not to limit students to a particular set of interpretations about their strengths or weaknesses based on what colors they see in meditation; rather, I use this tool as a way to guide their awareness to different parts of their body. This visualization of colors was effective for me, as the chakras' colors provided a road map of my own journey.

When I was making the decision about which program to attend for my doctoral work, I was debating between two schools. Even though I have an especially deep voice, at times I struggle to express my feelings. This was making my decision difficult.

I was feeling stuck, so I turned to meditation. At the time I just so happened to be attending the chakra retreat. In the chakra system the voice is represented by a counterclockwise-spinning vortex of blue. When I explored this color in meditation during the retreat, I discovered what I imagined to be blocks, almost like visual debris in my throat. I visualized it clearing away, and a sense of expansion as well as a strong urge to write overcame me.

After the retreat I sat some more with the decision I still had to make. I looked at the pamphlets from the two doctoral programs: one was green, the color of the heart, and the other was blue, the color of the voice. It seems like a silly reason to find direction or purpose in one's life, and I'm not saying this was the only factor in my decision, but I felt at this particular moment that the color blue was a very clear omen. After I made the decision, I ran into a close friend. When I announced that I was going to attend this particular program and university, their first response was "Go Blue!" It seemed to me to be a cosmic affirmation.

When I look back on my other educational experiences, I'm struck by how the colors of the chakras mirror my own learning. My high school's mascot was the Yellow Jackets, my college had a mascot called "Big Green," my graduate experience began at "Go Blue" and ended with a school whose color is violet. I'm not recommending that one make life choices based on colors, but again — color can be a powerful tool for student reflection.

In the workshop I ran for one of the school's Wellness Days, I introduced students to the broader color system of the chakras and then led them in a simple meditation on each color. So successful have I found this type of meditation to be that I often draw upon it in other contexts, and I use the visualization of color as an element in many of my weekly meditations.

When introducing the chakras, it is important to not impose a set of ideas about what the colors mean; simply ask students what colors they see and what they believe those colors mean before explaining the system. A student might connect a color to an emotional state, a set of circumstances they are facing in life, or nothing at all.

At the very least, community is created as students share their colors, and many connect with one another over shared colors. In more advanced settings with seasoned meditators, I even ask those present to look at their neighbor through their inner eye and see their energetic color. This can be a fun game that awakens a sense of playfulness. So much of what students do in the course of the school day is judged and labeled, and meditation can create a space free from seriousness or tension.

It isn't hard to imagine how a deeper understanding of each of the chakras can facilitate self-knowing, self-understanding, and self-insight. I would encourage anyone leading a workshop around the chakras to have many crayons and markers available afterward. I find that drawing a little stick figure and decorating it with the colors representing one's own chakras can be a very helpful tool of self-reflection for students.

CONCLUSION

There's a lot of apprehension, even fear, around working with teenagers. I often hear people saying teenagers are "jaded," "sarcastic," and "quick to dismiss and challenge anything an adult tells them." I'm sure any teacher who works with these students will tell you that these things are sometimes true, but that teenagers can also be joyful, honest, and models of vulnerability for adults struggling to be authentic. I've also found that teenagers have a very fine-tuned barometer for BS.

If what is being said isn't believed, embodied, or lived by the adult saying it, a teenager will sniff out the BS, and this turns out to be particularly true for anything pertaining to meditation. You have to have some kind of personal practice if you are going to be successful across all ages. When you have a certain level of experience and authenticity and have worked on creating a safe and nurturing space, you will find that high school students are capable of tapping into things far beyond what most people can imagine.

THE GRATITUDE MEDITATION

Place a lit candle three or four feet in front of you. Find a comfortable position on a chair or cushion. Make any adjustments you might need, rotate your shoulders, relax your arms, and let your legs be loose. When you are ready either lower your eyes into a soft forward gaze or, if you are comfortable doing so, close your eyes.

Take three breaths, and with each breath find yourself moving further and deeper into your body.

Let yourself fall into your body until you reach your heart center.

Imagine your heart is a room, any room, and in the center of this space is a beautiful candle.

As you see the candle in your mind's eye, move closer and closer to it with each breath until you find yourself only a few inches from this light.

Take a moment to observe this candle — the wick, the wax, the flame, all of the elements that represent your heart.

Take another deep breath. This time as you exhale, imagine you are blowing your breath into this candle. But this is a special candle. Imagine that with each exhale the light expands a little further. Continue to do this until the light from this candle has expanded to roughly the size of your body.

When you are ready, step into this light. Feel yourself lifted off the floor and out of your body. First you rise just a few feet, and then more, and more.

Take three more deep breaths and feel this light lifting you up and out of this room.

Take another deep inhale until you can see all of Earth. Let yourself be taken to the edge of your awareness, the edge of your creativity, the edge of your mind.

As you move out into space, look around and find a star. Let this be your star.

As you take your next breath, feel yourself being pulled toward this star.

Feel yourself moving closer and closer until the light of this star fuses with the light of your candle. Let this light fill your whole being.

Look around this star, and begin to see the faces of the other people who have been a part of your life. Feel the love of all those around you. Some of the faces you may recognize, some you may not. Feel the love, the pride, the joy they have for all you have done, all you do, and all you will do. Feel the love of their acceptance.

See in yourself what they see — an incredibly special being with love, light, gifts, and talents.

Take a moment and reconnect with them.

Fill your heart with all the love the people share, and then feel a well of gratitude filling up within your being.

Before you say goodbye, recognize that these special people are always with you.

Give them a final hug and wave.

Step back into that beautiful light of your candle.

Take a deep inhale, and feel yourself moving away from that star.

Take another deep breath, and feel yourself slipping back into your body.

Pause for a moment, and reconnect with that light in your heart.

Feel the well of gratitude that now resides in your being.

And then, and only then, take three long breaths, focusing on the exhale, and when you reach the final one, open your eyes.

CHAPTER EIGHT

❧❧❧

FIELD TRIPS

In 2015 I had the opportunity to take a group of students to Paris and London. We left school the first Friday night of spring break and spent the next eight days traveling across northern Europe. We visited museums and markets, we traveled on buses and trains, and we climbed to the top of the Tor in Glastonbury and walked through the narrow streets of Paris. But honestly, the experience that stood out for both me and many students occurred on the third day of the trip.

After spending two exciting days exploring Paris, my co-leader and I decided to take the students on an excursion to the place my wife and I had discovered years before, the small town of Chartres. It was only a ninety-minute train ride, which left us on the outskirts of the town. After a ten-minute walk up a hill to the town center, I found myself staring again at one of the most iconic medieval structures in the world. The cathedral is a marvel of stonework and glass, towering over 120 feet tall with two asymmetrical spires, one dedicated to the moon and the other dedicated to the sun. Three doorways, serving as royal portals in medieval times, welcome visitors in to the last remnant of the original Romanesque church. The stained-glass windows date back to the early thirteenth century — a collection unmatched anywhere in Europe that tells the history of the Christian world from the Garden of Eden to the Last Judgment. There are so many other impressive aspects of Chartres, discussed in countless books, but the feature that stood out on our trip was the medieval labyrinth inlaid on the stone slabs of the church floor.

The labyrinth is open for walking only on the first Friday of the month. The rest of the time it remains poorly hidden under the rows and rows of wooden chairs, where we now found our seats. Even with all the beauty surrounding us, I couldn't help but notice my eyes, and my students', being drawn down to the intricate pattern beneath our feet. The labyrinth at Chartres is a powerful symbol of the inner journey and just as relevant today as it was in the ancient world. While many like to describe it as a maze, in fact it is not a maze, but rather a single path with no wrong turns that draws the walker into its center.

FINDING THE DOORWAY TO THE HEART

The labyrinth, in Chartres and in almost every other place it is used, serves as a symbol of the path inward, a pilgrimage into the heart. Whether it is Moana returning the stone to Te Fiti or Theseus descending into the depths of the palace at Knossos, the labyrinth has come to symbolize the inner journey. Joseph Campbell captured this journey eloquently in his work *The Hero with a Thousand Faces*:

We have only to follow the thread of the hero-path. And where we had thought to find an abomination, we shall find a god; where we had thought to slay another, we shall slay ourselves; where we had thought to travel outward, we shall come to the center of our own existence; where we had thought to be alone, we shall be with all the world.[1]

The labyrinth is a symbol of this journey, and the cathedrals were structures intended to inspire this inner exploration, like so many sacred structures before and after them.

As we sat in Chartres, I could feel my students growing restless around me, a common feeling for any teacher. It was that moment when you know intuitively that something needs to change but you aren't really sure how to change it. That's when the real magic of teaching rises to the surface. Maybe it's time to show a clip you were saving for the next week, or to cut a lecture short and open up a discussion. In that instance, I knew I had to find a way to allow these students to access the power of this place. And quickly! Unfortunately, on field trips the unknown can feel even more pressing than the scramble to fill the last twenty minutes of class or the search for a handout you need before your next class starts. The unknown outside the classroom is literally out of sight — around the corner or on the other side of a building.

I knew we couldn't very well walk a labyrinth completely covered by chairs, but I also knew I didn't want to waste this opportunity. So I led the group quietly out of the building to get some perspective. The building stretches out across the equivalent of multiple football fields. As we walked we came around the back of the church, the ambulatory, where we found a little park and a bench. While I felt we were moving in the right direction, I knew this wasn't the perfect place for what I wanted to do. I led the students to the edge of this little area, where a small stone wall ran lengthwise. I peered over the wall to see beneath me, at a distance of only twenty feet or so, a tiered garden, resting upon the sloping hill descending away from the back of the cathedral. On the second tier was a wide grass lawn cut in the shape of...a labyrinth. Bingo.

I led the students down to this spot and, acting as if I'd planned this all along, encouraged them to make a circle on the ground in whatever way felt most comfortable. Here you can already see a distinction between in-class meditations and those you might lead on a trip. I would never have students lie down on their backs in the classroom, but here I placed comfort above structure. And while some chose to sit, many students lay down within the circle of the labyrinth and let the grass tickle their ears and the back of their necks. The only recommendation I made was that if the students did lie down, they place their heads in the center of the circle and their feet pointing out. I did this for two reasons: one, it energetically gave the students personal space and a channel (through their feet) by which to exhale their emotional baggage without sending it into another student. This is very similar to the way I would create a circle of chairs in the classroom, with a foot between each seat so students don't find themselves in another's field. But the arrangement had a second reason — and often a more practical one when you find yourself leading a meditation outside — and that is simply that it made it easier to be heard.

NOISE AND OTHER OUTDOOR CHALLENGES

One of the biggest challenges when meditating in a school building is external noise. Meditation leaders often feel like they are competing against the sounds all around them. Whatever the noises around you, make sure that students can hear your voice.

This raises an important point about leading a meditation outside: you have to be mindful of what you can control and let go of the rest. In the case of our meditation on the grounds of Chartres Cathedral, I chose the spot partly because it was secluded. But even in the most secluded spot in our modern world you might find yourself competing with airplane traffic or a nesting bird. The key, whether inside the classroom or on a field trip, is not to compete with these sounds but to use them as tools to deepen the meditation. You want your voice to be strong, but not forceful. You want your words to be heard, but not to be harsh.

I have to laugh though, because this balance isn't always perfect. During my third year of offering meditations in the classroom, some students begged me to take them outside for meditation. I finally agreed, but only if we held it on the last day of class. The day came, and students brought yoga mats and blankets to my classroom. Everyone seemed excited about the meditation. After going over a few final housekeeping issues, I led the class outside. They found comfortable spots on the school's front lawn, and we held the meditation. It wasn't great, because there was the constant noise of passing traffic and kids coming in and out of the building.

At the end of the meditation I gathered the class in a circle to share their experience. One student seemed really agitated.

He was swatting at things all over his body. I walked over to him and asked if he was okay. He lifted his mat and revealed a giant anthill. He had been too afraid to say anything during the meditation in case it might disturb the rest of the class, but the ants had been biting him the whole time. We both laughed, and I told him to go to the bathroom and make sure he got all the little creatures off. I appreciated his humor in light of the situation and learned a valuable lesson — not everything can be controlled.

THREE BREATHS

As the students at Chartres Cathedral settled into their positions all around me on the grass, some on their backs, others cross-legged, I made my way to the center of the circle. I encouraged everyone to make themselves comfortable. This is something I might caution against when meditating with adults, who are more likely to fall asleep on their backs, but teenagers, especially outside, will almost never fall asleep. I then invited them to close their eyes, and we began.

In almost all of my guided meditations I begin with three breaths, and I intentionally end with three long exhales. This simple process brings us all together as we start the meditation and joins us back together when we finally end, regardless of the individual journeys we take in between. Honoring the individual journey is very important, especially for young people, but the breath gives us continuity and a sense of community.

For the next twenty minutes I drew upon the symbol of the labyrinth and the energy of the landscape for inspiration as I guided the students in an exploration of their hearts. Throughout the meditation I continued to encourage them to move deeper and further inward. At the end of the meditation, regardless of how the students were facing or lying, I asked them to return to our circle, sitting up and facing forward.

In the classroom I would almost always encourage students to write a reflection before speaking about their experience, but on a field trip or when meditating outside they might not have any writing tools with them. That's okay. It just requires a little more patience on your part. Without the reflective writing exercise to get them started, sharing sometimes takes a little extra time.

In the case of this meditation, that is exactly what happened. It did take a little more time for the students to feel comfortable sharing their experience, and it required me to become more comfortable sitting with them in silence. But as the students began to share, one by one, the space and place began to work their magic. The students drew upon the surrounding imagery to share both the surprises and the secrets they had found residing in their hearts.

It is not uncommon for students to first share more of the physical experience of meditation, like "I heard the sound of birds" or "I felt the sun on my skin." But with some gentle questions and prodding, you can move them deeper into their hearts. Let everyone have a chance to share, even if it takes a long time. It is equally empowering to affirm their courage in sharing, with a simple "thank you" after each student's comments. Try not to let them view your feedback as evaluative or judgmental. Less is more with kids. A kind word of affirmation like "thank you" is all that is needed to open a deeply powerful conversation about their inner lives and worlds, while a word like "good" could connote the kind of judgment that is so prevalent in schools. Of course you should always allow students the option of passing, but you will be surprised at how rarely this occurs.

TURNING POINTS AND STUDENT VOICES

In the end, our meditation and reflection in the garden became a turning point on the trip. Before it was all over we meditated twice more, again in London and then in Glastonbury. Each meditation seemed to take us deeper into ourselves, but also to connect us as a group in unexpected ways. Our meditation offered a way to sit, reflect, and share our experiences in these places in a very personal way. At the end of the trip my co-leader and I sought to honor that contribution by giving each student a postcard with a word about what they had brought to the trip; for many, the word came directly from what they shared after the meditations.

Here is an excerpt from one student's journal, written after meditating at the top of the Glastonbury Tor:

Ascending the rickety wooden steps laid upon the steep incline, all I could do was allow myself to be utterly mesmerized by the sights of the land around me, ground that felt sacred.... The land below and beyond was every shade of green and stretched out on all sides for what seemed like forever.

The deeper my breaths grew, the more I could feel those spirits circulating through my body — seeming like they were trying to cleanse me. I felt so close to the sky that if I could reach out just a little farther I could grab it.... Each chakra during the meditation brought a new experience to mind.... I felt pain, happiness, anger, and gratitude with each new energy I heard about.... Lying on top of the Tor, I was sending love right out to every person and every space.... I felt deep connections to particular people in my life, but the setting, raised high above the English countryside with what felt like a whole world below me, made me want to send out as much love and gratitude as I could.

Natalie Knight
April 2015

Field trips, whether they are journeys across the Atlantic or simple walks outside the school building, offer students a new light in which to see each other and see themselves. So often we find ourselves pressured to justify any time spent outside the building, with an itinerary packed from top to bottom. However, without time to reflect, to process, and to share, almost none of the experience is ever internalized. There is something very powerful about stepping outside of the classroom to learn in the world around us. And there is something equally powerful about meditating in a group. It is truly amazing to see how transformative and healing these two things can be when brought together.

Meditating Outside

- **Find a quiet spot.** You can never fully escape the noise of the outside world, whether you are meditating outside or inside, but try your best.
- **Be aware of the sun.** If it is in the fall or early spring, the sun can be a great complement to a meditation, but if you lead a meditation in a warmer season,

try to find enough shade for everyone, as sitting in direct sunlight can become almost intolerable.

- **Take off your shoes.** I would encourage both you and the students to remove shoes and socks. This can create a great connection with the earth.
- **Avoid AstroTurf.** Try to find a space where the students can feel the earth beneath them, particularly if you are leading a grounding meditation. Sometimes it is nice if students bring towels or mats, but it isn't necessary.
- **Bring pencils and paper.** This makes it look to the random passerby like you are engaging in "academic" work, and it will also facilitate greater sharing after students reflect on the experience.

CONCLUSION

A simple thing we can all do to improve our sense of well-being and happiness is to just get outside a little more. The more often we connect with nature, the more often we are able to take a deep breath of fresh air, or a short walk into town, the better off we'll feel. The other day my class had just finished reading a piece on empathy. I was planning on leading them in a reflection on the article and getting their thoughts, when it suddenly hit me — why don't we do this outside? I told the students to grab their jackets and meet down in the courtyard.

As I think back on the conversation that followed, I'm not exactly sure how much of each other's comments the students got at first. It was a little difficult to hear out in the open, and it took a good five to ten minutes to just settle into this new space. But the longer we sat out there, the more I could feel a general sense of ease start to permeate the energy of the whole group. For one, it was an amazing morning, and the three trees in the courtyard were popping with autumn color, but for another, just the very act of getting outside of the classroom walls was a physically liberating and reenergizing experience.

I don't think spending every class discussion outside is the wisest use of one's teaching time, but I do think going outside at least once a quarter can be a really refreshing pedagogical tool. Of course some of the decisions to take your class outside will be spontaneous, but if you have a chance to plan, you might consider doing it at the end of the week, or the end of the quarter. At these moments students are much more open to reflection and introspection. You can certainly use this time to lead the students in discussions around relevant content and curriculum, but you can also use it as a space to reflect on the class as a whole. Moments like these can prove invaluable in developing a stronger sense of community among the students, and they can also give you valuable feedback for shifting or changing the class in ways that resonate with them.

THE HEART MEDITATION

Find a comfortable space on a chair or a cushion. First I ask you not to cross your arms or your legs. It's best if you just place your hands softly on your thighs, or wherever may be most comfortable. When you are ready, either lower your eyes and just stare with a soft gaze at the floor or the desk or, if you are comfortable doing so, close your eyes. When you are ready, take three breaths and begin.

Let the first few breaths be effortless and natural. Just observe your breath as one might watch a stream or a river.

Let the breath come in through your nose or your mouth.

As your breath begins to find its natural rhythm, shift your attention to your thoughts.

Imagine your thoughts are thick clouds floating across the sky. Maybe there are many, or maybe there are just a few. It doesn't matter either way, and there is nothing to judge — just watch and breathe.

With each breath, imagine that the space between the clouds is growing. Imagine that your exhale creates even more space and light between them.

When you are ready, turn your attention inward. Take a deep inhale and follow that breath into your heart space.

As you enter this sacred place, see if you can feel your heart beating. Imagine you can see it opening and closing.

Let the sound of this beating fill your ears and draw you deeper and deeper inside.

Imagine a path is stretched out before you, a path that leads into the center of your being.

See yourself walking that path — one step at a time, one breath at a time. As you move deeper, imagine you can see different objects on your path. Maybe some are memories, and some are dreams.

As you pass these objects, feel free to pause and look at them, but keep moving even deeper.

Let yourself walk farther and farther along this path. Imagine it spiraling in on itself like a beautiful flower or a labyrinth of stone.

As you approach the center, imagine you can see a light ahead, a fire. Who resides there? Who waits at the center of your heart? A friend, a relative, one who has come before you?

What wisdom and insight do they have to share with you? Listen closely. Their answer may come as a whisper, an image, or even an object.

See, feel, and breathe what they offer.

Hear your heart beating, feel your breath exhaling, and when you are ready take three long breaths and open your eyes.

CHAPTER NINE

᠆᠆᠆

TRAGEDY AND TRAUMA

Twice now I've walked into the school building and been greeted by grief-stricken students. Unfortunately, grief and loss are as much a part of the school experience as joy and celebration. If schools are microcosms of the world around them, this spectrum of experience and emotions shouldn't just be acknowledged, but also honored. And with the continued wave of violence and shootings in schools today, meditation should be embraced as a powerful force for transformation and healing in the lives of our students.

The first experience really spoke to me about the power of meditation in helping students process these emotions. It was in the middle of October, and I'd just begun my first period when the news began to spread about the death of a student. The young man had been in a hard collision while playing soccer the night before. He'd been rushed to the hospital, but the damage to his organs was so severe it led to rapid failure.

As the period progressed, the sound of crying students began to fill the halls. It was clear that the school was descending into a crisis situation, and the administration was struggling to handle the deteriorating climate. Twice during the period administrators came into the classroom, advising the class that any students who needed support services should head immediately down to the cafeteria. With this news the class took on a very somber feeling. As I did my best to strike a balance between the class content and the transpiring events, a third administrator came in. This time it was the assistant superintendent. She asked if she could speak to me privately out in the hall. Of course, I agreed and excused myself from the class after directing the students to read and respond to a short passage they'd been given earlier in the period. As I stepped out into the hall I could see that the assistant superintendent was deeply unsettled.

"Bill, we were wondering if you might be willing to lead a guided meditation for the students down in the cafeteria?"

"Of course," I responded without hesitation. "When would you like me to go down there?"

"Right now," she answered.

I paused. "Now?"

"Don't worry," she said, "We'll get someone to cover your class."

"Okay," I answered, although my fear wasn't about class coverage, but about what I was going to say or do. "I just need to use the bathroom first."

"No problem. I'll meet you down there."

I walked to the bathroom and splashed some cool water on my face. The largest meditation I'd ever led up to that point was a class of thirty students. I had no idea how many students were in the cafeteria, but I had a feeling it was far more than thirty. But even scarier was not knowing what I might say or do. As I've mentioned, it is very rare that I work from a scripted meditation, but I generally at least have a feeling of the direction I'd like to go or the images I might use. In this case, I had neither.

I took a deep breath and headed to the cafeteria. What I saw when I got there was even more overwhelming than what I had imagined. Well over 120 students were spread out across the room, some sobbing uncontrollably while others were in the corner crying quietly. And not only was it a very fraught situation, but I was trying to help people who didn't have any experience as meditators.

I made my way through the maze of students, tables, and backpacks strewn across the floor until I found a spot against the back wall. There was no way to make a circle in the space, and the hard plastic benches attached to the folding lunch tables made for some of the most uncomfortable seats one could imagine. At the same time, I knew I needed to claim the space in some way and shift the energy from chaos and tumult to something more orderly.

SPACE REVISITED

Multiple times in this book I've come back to this idea of claiming and organizing the space before a meditation. I really can't stress this enough. A great space can't itself make the experience, but a negative space can prevent the experience from deepening in the way one hopes. There is really no right or wrong way to claim the space or prepare for a meditation, but intentionality must be present before one begins.

From my spot against the back wall of the cafeteria, I asked the students to come forward and sit in a horseshoe shape as best they could around me. I did this for two reasons: one, I needed the students to hear me, and given the sprawling size of the cafeteria that wouldn't be possible in their current positions. And second, I wanted to combine the smaller groups that had formed as the administration rushed to get students into the cafeteria, and this horseshoe seating formation would create a more unified feeling for the meditation.

After all the students had settled into their new seats, I asked everyone to take three breaths and close their eyes. In another setting or set of circumstances I might have taken the time to have students sit up straight, square up their legs, or even roll their shoulders back, but at this time and in this place it didn't feel appropriate. This illustrates a key guideline. Just as I would encourage classroom teachers to always trust their feelings above what they are told they should or must do, I'd also tell meditation leaders the same when leading a meditation. Let the students inspire the experience, but let your intuition guide you in discerning what the students need at that moment.

As I asked the group to close their eyes, I closed my own. It didn't feel weird to close my eyes in front of all these students, but standing rather than sitting was a little awkward for me, as I'd always led meditations from a seated position and usually my palms would be down on my legs. In this situation I remained standing, and I turned slightly to face the entire group in a simple gesture of openness and connection.

I often close my eyes so that I can fully immerse myself in the experience while meditating with the students. And the images that come to my mind guide me in directing the meditation. It is a very intuitive process. This time, though, there were no clear images — just a thousand thoughts running through my head. I imagine that this was probably what the students were also experiencing as they closed their eyes. So I did what first surfaces whenever my mind is being overactive; I asked the students to ground their awareness in the breath and let that move their awareness out of their heads and into their hearts.

BREATH REVISITED

I began the grounding by having the students turn their attention to their breath. "Is it deep, or shallow?" I asked. "Is it quick, or slow?" I encouraged them to observe the breath without judgment, and through their observation, to begin to slow the inhale. A step that might have lasted only a minute or two in another setting, I stretched out for several minutes, allowing the communal breath to calm the space and the audible sound of crying to quiet. After I felt comfortable with their breath, as well as my own, I had the students turn their attention downward, to their feet.

Connecting with one's feet and the earth is a great way to ground the energy in the body and also to ground the experience. A good friend of mine, while going through her teacher training as a yoga instructor, made a commitment to place her bare feet on the earth every day over a nine-month period. Rain, snow, or shine, she made her way outside and stood on the earth for a few minutes. I was so struck by this simple but powerful exercise. Today it is rare that we ever touch the earth directly, and it is even rarer for many of our students, as their grass fields are replaced by plastic and AstroTurf. This connection to the earth is our connection with self and center.

Many students over the years have shared with me that they tend to be drawn to images of the beach when meditating. I think there are many reasons for this, including the rhythmic motion of the waves, which mirrors that of the breath. But also, the ocean is one of the few places that we can walk barefoot. I have learned to use this powerful image and sensory memory to encourage students to feel their feet sinking into the sand, just as they would at the edge of the ocean.

This particular meditation was more about grounding than opening upward. But I want to point out that just as students have lost their connection to the earth, they have also lost a connection to the stars. I remember a consultant who visited my school explaining that students do their best thinking when they can look out a window and see a space of greater than twenty feet. This idea of daydreaming or staring into space has been deemed a counterproductive activity in schools, when in fact science has proven it is the very opposite.[1]

These moments of staring into space are actually the times when we best process the information we have been given, or make sense of the thoughts swirling in our heads. Even more powerful are the opportunities to stare at the horizon, as we might while on a mountain or standing on a beach. And even more powerful to the expansion of the unconscious are those opportunities to stare into space and see the vastness of the universe that surrounds us. Just as important as one's connection to the earth is one's connection to the stars — an image utilized in an earlier meditation of this book but also a theme I'll revisit at the end.

THE HEART SPACE

Slowly, without force, I asked the students to drop their attention, along with their breath, into their hearts. So much resides in the heart, and whenever we delve into this place we are certain to be dipping into deep waters. In our hearts we hold memories, wounds, unresolved emotions, and often our joys with friends and family members.

As we entered this space, I imagined many of the students were tapping into the grief and heartbreak they were experiencing, and this was made even more apparent by an increase in crying. I didn't want them to whitewash or bury this experience, but rather to connect with it. I asked the students to imagine a space where they felt very safe — maybe a bedroom or a grandparent's house or even a place in nature. I like to call this "the heart space," a place that resides within all of us both physically and spiritually. In this space I encouraged them to look around and explore, hoping the memory would have a calming and comforting effect. I then encouraged the students to notice a candle resting somewhere in the space. I invited them to observe the wax, the wick, and the flame. "May this be a symbol of your heart at this moment," I said.

I then encouraged them to imagine another candle appearing in the space, representing someone they cared for dearly. Then another. One by one, I continued this visualization, adding candles until they could imagine a room full of light, like a constellation of stars surrounding them. And then I cued them to breathe three breaths. I invited them to breathe as if they were breathing the light of all the candles into their heart, their feet, their fingertips, and the center of their being. Drawing on this image of a candle (or a ball of light or simply an orb) is an especially valuable method when students are struggling or dealing with strong emotions, as it can often help clear and transform challenging thoughts and emotions into something manageable and healing.

After this exercise, I had all the students open their eyes. As I looked around I encouraged them to return to that place within their hearts over the next days, weeks, and months whenever they felt overwhelmed by their emotions or needed to hold the space for another to deal with their emotions. There were still faces wet with tears and some students were still crying, but a shift had occurred. What was once overwhelming seemed a little less so. The administrator thanked me and I returned to my room, both exhausted and at the same time inspired by what I'd just experienced.

I share this story not to suggest that meditation is the answer to all students' emotional turbulence but to illustrate how empowering it is to honor students' feelings as part of the learning and grieving process. Reconnecting to the heart and the emotional lives of students is a part of deep and meaningful learning. Often we shy away from discussing grief or loss in the classroom, and in the process we are failing to honor a part of our students' lives. Whether it is through meditation, journaling, or a simple conversation, we must bring the emotional needs of our students to the front of our classrooms.

Teachers can help students become more attuned to what stress feels like in the body as it rises and falls. Some meditation practitioners like to call this "checking the weather" or "checking the stress thermometer" of the emotional body. Remember that students, especially younger ones, might not have the tools or capacity to deal with stress in the same ways that we can as adults. Meditation is a wonderful tool for dealing with stress in a healthy way. It first helps students identify the stress they are feeling, and then it offers a way to move through it. These practices don't get rid of pain and suffering, but they do provide a compassionate space for them to exist in.

Teaching is a balance of planning and spontaneity. I'm sure to some extent this balance exists in every profession, but there is something especially unique about the classroom environment. It often is outside the lesson plan that something truly transformative and magical takes place. When I walked into school that day I wasn't planning on leading a grade-wide meditation on grief — I wasn't even planning on leading any meditations — but something opened and the opportunity presented itself. This flexibility throughout the school day is something that meditation nurtures within the brain. Ninety percent of our days are very predictable, and certain activities often repeat day in and day out, or even year in and year out. But it is that last 10 percent that gives life meaning. In the classroom, it's found in the willingness to let go of the obsession with the outcome, the test scores, and the lesson plans at the expense of the students. Making time for a student, valuing the journey over the end goal, can change a life.

Dealing with Trauma

- **Never rush a student.** This seems obvious, but it is very challenging. If you are on your way to a meeting and come across a troubled student in the hall, patience must still prevail. Once a student feels rushed, particularly around deeply personal topics, they will shut down.

- **Follow up.** You should always follow up with students who appear troubled, but more importantly you need to reach out to their parents, guidance counselors, and the administration. You would be surprised how often meditations reveal deep-seated issues that a student has been struggling with for

years, yet no one has noticed or was notified about
it at the school.

- **Be a mandated reporter.** Always be open, honest,
and supportive with students, but make them aware
from the start of your conversation that you are a
mandated reporter, and if anything they reveal to
you puts them or another in danger you will have
to notify an administrator. You never want to explain this after an intense conversation rather than
before. They will feel betrayed, and your relationship with them, which could be crucial to facilitating a future resolution, will be shattered.

CONCLUSION

There are times when meditation awakens something that is
simply too overwhelming for a student to handle. I have seen
this happen on several occasions. Sometimes it happens when
a student taps into challenges they are experiencing at home
or an unidentified past trauma. Whenever I become aware that
this has happened during a meditation, I approach the student
at the end and check in with them to see if they are okay. It
would be a rare instance if they decided to immediately open
up, but I follow these kids closely over the next months and
stay in close communication with their guidance counselors.
Following up on these moments is so crucial to creating a safe
and healthy environment for all students.

Especially when delving into visual meditation, one has to
be aware and mindful of how students might react and what
could surface in the process. Honoring students' decision to
share or not and then giving them the space to reflect and the
time to process their experience creates a healthy environment.

THE CANDLE MEDITATION

Place a lit candle three or four feet in front of you. Find a comfortable position on a chair or cushion. Make any adjustments you might need, rotate your shoulders, relax your arms, and let your legs be loose. When you are ready, either lower your eyes into a soft forward gaze or, if you are comfortable doing so, close your eyes. Take three breaths and begin.

With each breath, feel yourself falling deeper and further into your body.

If it helps, imagine that with each inhale you are dropping deeper into a warm pool of water.

Let your legs, your arms, and your head dissolve into this liquid. Let your thoughts and your feelings go.

Take another deep breath and begin to feel your body, from skin to bones, from feet to head, floating in this space. Now turn your gaze inward.

Take another deep breath and drop into your heart space. If it helps, imagine yourself walking into a room. In the center of this room, picture a candle. Walk up to this candle, notice the color of the flame, the wick, and the wax. Notice what this candle is resting on. Walk around this candle and observe the perfections and imperfections that make it so unique. Feel a sense of gratitude for the light that comes from this candle.

Sit down across from this candle.

Notice how the flame expands and contracts like the beating of your heart.

As you look around, begin to notice other candles surrounding you.

One by one, let these candles represent the people in your life and the people you have touched. Each candle may be different, each one representing the uniqueness of that individual.

Now imagine drawing the light of those candles into your own heart with your inhalation. Feel yourself expand and lighten.

Take another deep breath, and feel a well of gratitude for all the light around you and all the light you have brought to others.

Pause for a moment, and return back to *your* candle. Imagine yourself reaching out and placing that candle in your heart. Feel a sense of warmth fill you.

And then, and only then, take three long breaths, focusing on the exhale, and when you reach the final one, open your eyes.

CHAPTER TEN

❧❧❧❧❧

ELEMENTARY SCHOOL

Questions are the bread and butter of any great classroom. They feed the soul of the class and of the teacher. I can remember countless times when a simple but sincere question about the material would reawaken my own interest in and energy with the subject. When students ask questions it makes you realize that they are actually listening, that they are actually interested in learning more about the topic and thinking about it in new ways. As teachers it's so pedagogically valuable to create spaces and time for students to think about material and develop their own questions. To me, this is one measure of a successful classroom, maybe even more than any single score or test the students will ever take. But it's not something that just happens. Just as we test students out of their curiosity and creativity for learning, we can also teach them back into their questions.

THIRD GRADE AND MS. AIRES

Last year, I was walking down the hall to my classroom and saw that the third-grade bulletin board was filled with beautifully drawn prints of circles, triangles, and squares, all creating a tapestry of perfectly symmetrical designs. Later that day I ran into the teacher of that third-grade classroom and asked what her class was up to. She explained that they were just finishing a unit on symmetry and that the prints were part of the students' final projects. I loved it, and asked if she'd like me to come in and talk to the students about symmetry in history. Without so much as a blink she responded, "That'd be great."

A week later, I found myself in this third-grade classroom armed with a batch of PowerPoint images to share with the students on symmetry and history. There was so much I could talk about, so I decided to focus primarily on ancient Egypt and the treasures found in King Tut's tomb, just as my grandfather had shared with me when I was about the same age. One of the powerful lessons I've learned as a teacher is that often the story is just as significant as the content. The learning comes when one can connect the students to the material through a great story.

I walked into the classroom, set up the PowerPoint, then looked out at the room full of wide-eyed little eight-year-olds. I introduced myself, and then I began to tell them of the discovery of King Tut's tomb. The story is great because it is full of mystery, with a little magic, and even better yet, a curse. Now I don't really know if the curse of King Tut is real, but sometimes you need to leave a little space for wondering when working with younger audiences. So I told the whole story, and I then used that as a transition to sharing with them images of all the artwork and artifacts that were found in the tomb. With each image I asked the students to identify the symmetry, as well as the asymmetry. I asked them to consider the colors and the material, but most of all I wanted them to think about why the Egyptians were so drawn to making things symmetrical, even if that meant making them less realistic. This was all they needed to explode into a sea of waving hands, comments, and questions.

In so many ways that simple, twenty-minute lesson embodied much of what we teachers do on a larger scale: tell a story, create a space for questions, and connect students back to their curiosity. That to me is at the core of great teaching, and unfortunately, it's often something we lose over the years, as students get older. No longer do they have this deep sense of wonder. Rather, they approach learning as a means to an end, an end that either comes in the form of a grade on a test or an acceptance letter in the mail. Awakening the classroom isn't just about creating a greater sense of presence and life, but also about using this space to foster wonder and curiosity.

When I think about that third-grade class, I'm reminded of my own experience in third grade, with our teacher, Ms. Aires. I vividly remember the hours we spent reading on the classroom carpet after lunch, and the time Ms. Aires cried when Wilbur died in *Charlotte's Web*.[1] I remember the giant castle she had us build after reading *The Whipping Boy*.[2] But I also remember that there was always time to ask questions. We never felt rushed to the next topic or assignment. There wasn't an endless drumbeat of content, or the feeling of pressure from knowing we had fallen behind other students or classes. In Ms. Aires's room there was a clear and deliberate effort to create space and meet us in our own time.

As we go forward in this book, I want us to think about the

message we are sending students, the message about what is and what isn't important, and some of the deeper consequences of this unending drive for test prep. I want us to figure out how we can reconnect our eighteen-year-olds to the curiosity and wonder of our eight-year-olds, how we can awaken a deeper sense of wonder and love for learning within them, and how they can once again learn to ask authentic and genuine questions.

At the heart of the classroom should reside the students. Unfortunately, with a growing set of policies to correct "failing" schools, teachers find themselves balancing the needs of their students against the professional demands of the outside world. These demands can range from test prep for state and national exams to lockdown drills and growing concerns about school safety. The cost of all of this is the marginalization of students' emotional and inner needs. This chapter intends to reframe those needs and find a place for meditation in the classroom, whether it is for elementary students or seniors in high school.

While the majority of my career has been in a high school classroom, I've been fortunate to work in a K-12 building and find myself sharing the halls with students of all ages. This has also afforded me the opportunity to bring meditation into these classrooms just as I have into my own. And from this I've gained several very beneficial insights into the needs of students across a spectrum of ages and development.

LEADING MEDITATIONS IN ELEMENTARY SCHOOL

My first experience of meditating in the elementary school began several years after Meditation Club was formed. I mention this because it was the president of the club at the time who pushed the idea of bringing meditation into the younger grades. With her help we convinced the teachers to allow us to pioneer a five-week meditation program with the fifth grade, where a pair of high school students was assigned to each of the five fifth-grade classrooms, which they would visit once a week over a five-week period.

We got the approval of the teachers and administrators very easily, as they had noticed disturbing trends in the levels of stress and anxiety their students were reporting. I think the growing popularity of mindfulness in the education lexicon also piqued their interest. On my end, identifying ten high school students from Meditation Club who were excited to work with the younger students was also fairly easy. The real challenge was developing the curriculum for the students to teach. We had no idea how to begin, as none of us had ever worked with students so young.

I gathered the high school students in my classroom during lunch one day and we began brainstorming. The students shared a variety of ideas for the weekly lessons, from body scans to the creation of a class mandala. I thought the ideas sounded great, but I felt it was important to develop an arc for the curriculum and honor the three tenets of teaching meditation in school:

1. Introduce
2. Experience
3. Reflect

The students all agreed, and we came up with a curriculum that started with body scans, delved into inner visualizations, and ended with a collective activity, ideas for which ranged from creating a mandala to painting a class labyrinth on the front lawn of the school. We also agreed that each lesson would be built around a different theme. These would include happiness, gratitude, empathy, compassion, and reflection. The curriculum was now set, and all the students had to do was put it to work.

CHANGES AND REVISIONS TO THE PRACTICE WITH YOUNGER KIDS

After the first week, the high school students got back together and shared their experiences from the fifth-grade classrooms. Immediately several insights became clear to me. First, the meditation needed to be both mentally and physically engaging. The opening activity needed to switch from telling to asking. Questions should be the driving force in bringing to the surface student background knowledge and understanding around themes like compassion, gratitude, and happiness as well as how these related to the students' lives. The more the fifth graders had the opportunity to share their own experiences and thoughts, the better. The meditation leaders weren't there to lecture, but to guide — something very different from their own high school classes and experiences.

Second, before starting the meditation there needed to be some physical preparation. This could be rearranging desks or chairs, but we also agreed to a set of simple stretches to prepare the body for meditation. These included an arm stretch that had students flexing their wrists up and down, as well as a forward bend where students let their heads hang heavy over their legs. A simple twist from right to left to awaken the body was also added. Honestly, these stretches could be used at any age and serve a great purpose of awakening the body as students spend more of their days seated at desks.

Third, I let the meditation leaders craft their own meditations, both scripted and unscripted. We found this very successful. Rather than expecting me to tell them what to say, they each constructed an authentic dialog that they could take ownership of. Just as a teacher can't teach another's lesson, a meditation leader can't lead another's meditation.

As the fourth and final piece, we implemented a reflective activity that we agreed to do across the whole group. This group activity was a way for students to reflect and process the experience. There was a silent component, and also a space for sharing. In these activities students created journals, drew pictures, wrote letters, told stories, and created a class mandala.

STUDENT FEEDBACK

The feedback from our program revealed it to be a resounding success. The high school students and the elementary school students created friendships, a by-product of such deep reflection, and the teachers were eager to have the high school students back the next year. The only negative feedback was about the length of the program, with many teachers reporting that five weeks was not enough time to make a lasting impact. When we came back the next year, we added four more weeks and two additional themes: empathy and service.

Here are some of the comments we received from the fifth-grade students after running the program:

"It calms you after a long day."
"I found value in closing my eyes and imagining different things that helped me with my everyday life."

"I learned how to not feel overwhelmed with homework."

"I have learned how to forgive my friends."

"You taught me to just stop and breathe and stretch and
get back to what I am doing."

"...the relief of silence..."

"I relax and let my thoughts drift free."

"Meditation has helped me relax and put myself in a
different environment."

"I love taking out stress, and instead of hitting or at-
tacking, I meditate."

"I have learned how to empty my mind and to relax.
Now, I close my eyes and breathe in and out. I can
think about what has happened to me and I can find
peace."

"We are learning how to handle next year's stress."

"When I am mad, I take a deep breath."

"I have learned to try and pull myself into another
world."

"Before presentations, I now meditate....I felt relaxed
and that a weight was lifted off my shoulders."

"I thought the most valuable part was being able to
get away from the loudness of school and relax for
a bit."

As this feedback clearly shows, meditation has great benefits for young kids. From the mundane benefits, like getting
away from the sounds of school, to the more profound, like
forgiving a friend, the practice meets students exactly where
they are both developmentally and emotionally. However, I
have learned that this is possible only when you foster a sense of

openness in the practice. In an age when students are constantly inundated with information and entertainment, helping them access their knowledge, their feelings, or their imagination in a way that leaves a lasting impression is worth the energy.

Four Things to Remember When Meditating with Younger Kids

1. Keep the meditations simple.
2. Begin with a fun stretch or movement exercise to engage the whole body. Kids spend a lot of time sitting in the classroom, and you don't want to reinforce the notion that meditation is also a passive activity. By engaging the body, you can help students activate their minds.
3. Play with imagery, like shapes, colors, candles, stars, and hearts. Younger kids love these images and often tap into an endless source of creativity when meditating with them.
4. After the meditations, instead of having students write down their reflections, put out crayons or markers and let them draw the images.

CONCLUSION

I learned a lot from that experience with the fifth grade, particularly as it related to meditation with younger students. First, young kids can easily drop into a meditation in ways that adults can't, and they seem a lot more willing to go along for the journey, no matter the direction you take them. They are a lot more familiar with their imaginations than older students, which also might be a commentary on our classrooms and what we are asking older students to do compared with their younger peers. Younger kids are far more comfortable closing their eyes and trusting the facilitator than older students, who approach everything with a hefty dose of skepticism. Second, younger kids almost never laugh or giggle during a guided meditation, something older students often do as a defense mechanism. Lastly, offering an engaging activity after a meditation helps the students process the experience. While older students are usually happy to process their experience by simply writing in a journal or a notebook, younger students need to color, draw, and even cut out images. This tangible part of the process is so important to the integration and sharing of the meditation with the class.

I have found color to be a very simple but powerful tool in cultivating imagery with younger students. This tool is especially powerful when connected to the heart, and it can be an entry point to exploring complex concepts with ease in a way they might not otherwise be capable of. So often we take the view that the classroom is a space for finding answers, but in reality our best lessons and units lead students to more questions than they first began with. In these lessons we spark in students a deeper sense of knowing, and a deeper desire to know. It is clear that meditation is a powerful tool for facilitating this type of learning.

For meditation to take hold and have an impact on students' lives it has to offer something tangible. Students must find a benefit if they are going to return to it again and again. While adults might be less open at first, they tend to be more patient and polite about the results. With kids, especially young kids, if it doesn't help them *now* (to sleep better, deal with stress, clear their minds), they'll soon be moving on to the next thing. As

I've said before, placing students in a leadership role is crucial to the success of any initiative, and as I reflect on my experience using meditation in the classroom I'm always amazed at what students are able to accomplish and do themselves. Their initiative and ingenuity far surpass my own; all I need to do is just instill confidence in them and they come to life.

A UNIT PLAN FOR ELEMENTARY SCHOOL STUDENTS

This is an overview of a simple five-day unit that might introduce students from third to eighth grade to meditation. At some point early on, it may be helpful to have the students just close their eyes for a few minutes. This will help them get accustomed to the idea of sitting still with their eyes closed. The meditation themes of days two through four do not have to take place in any particular order; the teacher can choose the order. In addition to the oral reflection and discussion done immediately after the sessions, it may be helpful to have the students keep journals about their thoughts and experiences while meditating. A mandala activity, included in the appendix, can be a nice way to end the unit.

First Day

- Have students sit in a circle. Discuss the idea of stress relief through "being conscious" or "being aware."
- Lead some simple stretches, such as twisting the torso, rolling the shoulders back, kneading the hands.
- Explain the importance of stretching and posture, and have students take a proper sitting position (sitting up straight, but still comfortable).
- Lead a very short meditation session with the students (no more than two minutes) in which they practice being aware and present in the moment. This is a great place for the "Breath Meditation."
- Guide them through a "mental scan" of their body, having them pay attention to and then relax one body part at a time.

- After meditation, ask students to reflect on the experience:
  - ○ Do they feel any different?
  - ○ Was it difficult to concentrate or keep their eyes closed?

Days Two through Four

- Follow the setup and stretching routines from the first day.
- Lead a meditation session using one of the following themes: tree, river, or light.
  - ○ The tree meditation should focus on planting roots and extending branches, then drawing energy from the earth and the sky.
  - ○ The river meditation should focus on imagining the mind as a stream and letting one's thoughts flow peacefully.
  - ○ The light meditation should focus on picturing internal light that illuminates, cleanses, and calms the body.
- The sessions should gradually increase in length as the students gain experience and become more accustomed to meditation.
- Have the students reflect on and discuss their experiences after each meditation.

Last Day

- Follow the setup and stretching routines from the previous days.

- The last meditation session should focus on finding refuge within one's mind and being comfortable with the self.
- Emphasize the idea that relieving stress through meditation is a skill that the students can use in their own lives outside these sessions.
- Have the students reflect on and discuss their experiences as they did on previous days.

THE CHAKRA MEDITATION FOR KIDS

Find a comfortable position on a chair or cushion. Make any adjustments you might need, rotate your shoulders, relax your arms, and let your legs be loose. When you are ready, either lower your eyes into a soft forward gaze or, if you are comfortable doing so, close your eyes. Take three breaths and begin.

Inside your head is a world to discover.

Imagine yourself in a forest, walking along a path.

The path wanders through trees, over streams, and up a tall mountain.

At the top of the mountain you find yourself in a clearing.

Above you is the sun, and beneath you is the soft grass.

What do you see?

Can you see the red of the fallen maple leaves?

Imagine the color and breathe it in.

Can you see the orange of the slippery salamander?

Imagine the color and breathe it in.

Can you see the yellow of the bright sun?

Imagine the color and breathe it in.

Can you see the green of the thick forest?

Imagine the color and breathe it in.

Can you see the blue of the vast sky?

Imagine the color and breathe it in.

Can you see the indigo of the swaying irises?

Imagine the color and breathe it in.

Can you see the violet of a passing butterfly?

Imagine the color and breathe it in.

Take a deep breath, and now breathe in *all* the colors.

Can you see the rainbow of colors swirling within you?

Imagine the colors and exhale them out through the top of your head and the bottom of your feet.

And then, and only then, take three long breaths, focusing on the exhale, and when you reach the final one, open your eyes.

CHAPTER ELEVEN

〜〜〜〜〜

TEACHERS

Meditation shouldn't be reserved for students alone. Rather it should be a practice available to the whole school, including teachers, administrators, and parents. If adults are not included in the energetic shift of the school, then no interventions, new policies, or other positive changes will be lasting. And as stressed and overwhelmed as students are at times, so too are the adults. The adults, particularly teachers and parents, set the energetic tenor of the school.

Teaching is an incredible calling, and it doesn't just call your mind or your heart, it calls every part of your being. Every teacher will tell you this. Look around at your friends or your neighbors — while others can go out after work during the week or maybe stay up late watching TV, not so with us teachers. When you are teaching, you are drawing upon every part of who you are — your emotional well-being, your spiritual center, your heart, and your mind. And you are also working with every aspect of every student. To ignore your needs or the emotional needs of the students is to neglect a significant part of the classroom.

VOCATION

While many experiences and questions in my life pointed me toward teaching, I adamantly fought this calling as something that was antiquated, beneath me, and "something I'd never do because this is what my mom did." It's not hard to understand the deep aversion many young people have to teaching when we consider the larger societal discourse around education as a field that is broken, in disrepair, and hopelessly lost. It's a small miracle that people still consider teaching at all. However, those that do are a special breed. They feel that calling deep inside. And in my own experience the persistent call within my heart to teaching eventually drew me to the classroom, just as the persistent call to learning led me to the Camino de Santiago.

Meditation offers not only students but you as their teacher the ability to hear that quiet voice in your heart. Sometimes it speaks through words, other times it speaks through images, and most often, it speaks through feelings. Find the space to be open to those messages that bubble up from the subconscious. Living a life that honors that voice is what gives the work of teaching meaning.

The Latin root of the word *vocation* is *vocare*, "to call." In many ways our actions speak far more loudly and clearly of who we are than our words do. When you think about the classroom and the teacher's voice, you know that some voices are gentle and give students space, while some fill the space and suffocate students. One of the most disheartening things in the world is the feeling some students have that there is no space for them. That space to voice oneself is something we all have a right to, and creating a classroom where there is space for ideas, for learning, for beliefs, and for each individual is the groundwork for a transformative and self-realizing environment.

From the minute we come into this world we are learning, and eventually we model our own knowledge for others. In our best moments as teachers we bring our whole selves into the classroom, consciously and with intention. Throughout this book many themes and ideas connected to meditation have been discussed — space, voice, stillness, and silence — but the one theme I think is most important to the work, especially with adults, is happiness. Happiness is a simple concept, but a powerful force. Happiness is what draws us back to our hearts and the aspects of ourselves that make us most human. Teachers, especially, have an impetus to connect to that inner happiness, as it both reenergizes and renews us as professionals.

A COURSE FOR FACULTY

In 2013 I proposed a course for our faculty titled "The Enlightened Teacher." This course was structured into eight modules. Below is the original description of the course that was emailed out to the faculty.

Course Description

With the ever-growing politicization of education through mandated testing, standardized curriculums, and outcome-based systems of teacher evaluation, it appears as though we have forgotten what is most important in schools today, students and teachers. This workshop was inspired by my own work as an educator and my desire to return to the heart of what it means to teach and be taught. This workshop is presented in eight modules created to reexamine the basic elements of teaching and learning. The modules include story, intention, intuition, happiness, voice, mindfulness, creativity, and compassion. Each class will offer participants an opportunity to reflect, as well as to access transformative tools that will inform their daily teaching and curriculum. Through this workshop, each participant will have an opportunity to reevaluate their own understanding of themselves, both as educators in the 21st century and as members of a global teaching community.

As I look back at the description of the course I realize both how ambitious it was, but also how striking. I wanted to create a course that tapped into what I believed were foundational elements of teaching. Even though I knew that this description might turn some teachers away from taking the course, I believe it is important to be honest when engaging in this work. I didn't want any surprises for the faculty who enrolled.

The First Meeting

The director of professional development in the district asked me to introduce the course to the faculty at the next after-school staff meeting. I agreed, thinking I'd just be speaking for a couple of minutes, and was surprised to discover a day before the faculty meeting that the high school principal had slated me to speak for the last forty minutes. A little unnerved and a lot overwhelmed, I agreed.

The meeting started uneventfully, with an agenda covering the usual litany of business and housekeeping. After the principal touched on the order of business around schedule changes, upcoming drills, and the next conference day, he turned to me. I hesitantly got up and made my way to the front of the room. I looked over at the clock on the wall; there were still fifty minutes left in the meeting. I took a deep breath, swallowed to clear my throat, and began.

I'm not really sure what I said in the first ten minutes. I imagine it was something about the upcoming course and my inspiration for offering it. It wasn't long, though, before I began to see teachers growing disengaged. From the number of cell phones appearing and the papers shuffling on laps, I realized I was losing the entire room's attention.

Over the years I've found that some of the best teachers are the most impatient students. They need to be constantly engaged, and in this case I knew I had to do something to recharge the staff or the last thirty minutes would be a disaster. I stopped my presentation and asked everyone to close their laptops, put away their papers, and turn off their phones. The room was too crowded to create a circle, so I had all the teachers push their chairs back from the conference table so each person could have a little space. I then took another deep breath and closed my eyes.

It was by far the most difficult and nerve-wracking meditation I've ever guided. I think this was a reflection of both the initial resistance of the teachers and also the challenge of speaking in front of one's peers. As I mentioned earlier, I almost never know exactly what I'm going to say when leading a meditation; I just have a guiding idea or theme giving me direction. With this group the word that came to mind was *happiness*. The result was a guided meditation on school, teaching, and happiness. At the end of the meditation I asked the staff to open their eyes and write a short reflection. The reflection could be from the meditation or anything that came to mind during the session. Then I opened the floor to sharing.

If you think teenagers are resistant to sharing, just imagine the resistance of adults, especially adults at a faculty meeting. Fortunately, several teachers I was especially close with volunteered to share their thoughts. A few mentioned their classrooms, one mentioned his colleagues, and another described a small moment in the hall with a student. It wasn't long before these volunteers started a snowball of participation, as one teacher after another began sharing a moment of happiness from their life as an educator. The final twenty minutes passed effortlessly. As the rest of the room shared, there were so many different responses, from stories about mundane moments in the classroom to stories of returning alumni.

In retrospect, one story really stands out to me. After all the teachers shared their reflections, I turned to the principal and asked if he'd like to speak about a moment of happiness in the school. Dead silence. Finally, after a good thirty seconds, he shared a story of a young man he'd helped many years before, while teaching in another state. I waited another moment and then wrapped up the conversation just as the clock turned four. One month after the meeting, the principal announced his retirement. It seems a poignant illustration: when we lose the love for this work it is difficult to find the energy or enthusiasm to continue on.

The Enlightened Teacher

Meditation is not about changing minds, but it can help us connect with hearts. It can reveal what we have always known and felt. It can remind us of dreams that we have forgotten. So it was with the Enlightened Teacher course, which began with twelve teachers. Much of the model I used in the faculty meeting was repeated with this group, as over the next eight sessions we participated in a weekly meditation. We also read articles, listened to podcasts, and watched YouTube videos around each week's themes. But the meditations were by far the most powerful force in the course.

Halfway through, I began offering the meditation at the start of class as an opening activity instead of at the end. This change totally shifted the direction and energy of the group. I realized that teachers carry just as much distraction and worry into the room as kids. If I didn't take time to clear it with an opening meditation, it seemed to bog everything else down. Shifting the meditations to the start of the workshop allowed the teachers to clear the earlier experiences of the day and really tap into their hearts in the present.

After this course, a series of dominoes fell that have expanded the work's impact, as well as the interest of the staff, over the years since. That summer, the district agreed to send a cohort of teachers to a conference on mindfulness and education at the Omega Institute. The next year we continued the work of the Enlightened Teacher, this time running the meetings at lunchtime, with different teachers facilitating the conversation in their own room space. The faculty interest expanded beyond the high school to include staff across the full K-12 spectrum. Teachers began showing up at Meditation Club, and secretaries from the district office also came to participate. The chair of the social studies department asked me to open the department meetings with a weekly meditation. We created a book study around Thich Nhat Hanh's work *Happy Teachers Change the World*,[1] with participants from neighboring schools joining us. I gave a presentation to a group of retired teachers. And just this past year we opened the school year with a day of yoga and meditation for the middle and high school faculty.

Shifting the culture of the school is a whole-school effort. It's not just about the students, or the teachers — it's about the entire school. Meditation can address so many needs, from stress reduction to reflection to goal setting. It offers clarity of vision and clarity of voice. It's not just something for ending the semester — it's about opening and supporting growth throughout the year. It allows all members of the school community to be more engaged in their work.

INTEGRATING MEDITATION AND PREPARING TO LEAD

The world is filled with distractions and noise. We struggle to communicate with our neighbors, our families, and most of all, ourselves. When was the last time you considered what ignites your passions and joys? How long has it been since you took the time to tap into those dreams, those passions, those loves that *are* who you really are?

As we race to keep pace with the rapidly changing world around us, we move farther and farther away from the interior. Success, to-do lists, and obligations have taken precedence over our own sense of well-being and happiness. When you are most alive and full of energy as a teacher, then you are happy. And when your students are most alive, full of energy, and open to learn, then they are happy. If we are truly going to transform other people's lives, we have to start with our own; if we are going to transform our own lives, we have to reconnect with who we are. I believe that at the heart of who we are, and who our students are, we are beings of joy and happiness. Meditation is what helps us to uncover that joy.

Before leading others in meditation, first establish a personal practice. I would also encourage you to think about the other forces that shape a successful meditation. Get a good night's sleep the night before, maybe going to bed a little earlier, abstaining from alcohol for at least twenty-four hours, and really trying to eat a diet big on greens and low in meat. I'm not a dietitian or a physician, but I've found the physical and emotional prep for visual, or content-based, meditations begins long before one actually sits down with the students.

When I think about diet as it relates to meditation I follow a simple rule: fewer blacks and whites, and more greens. This means drinking green tea in the morning instead of coffee and avoiding processed foods, white flour, and sugar. In general, I find that a simple diet helps me feel more centered and balanced. The caffeine piece is particularly worth considering because coffee tends to overstimulate the conscious mind at the expense of the subconscious mind. While the conscious mind is often loud and constantly demands our attention, the subconscious is quiet and speaks in whispers. For its presence to be felt, it must be honored, and the conscious mind quieted.

PRESCRIPTION FOR TEACHING TEACHERS

Here are some recommendations for running a meditation or facilitating a group discussion with teachers. This is the format I've used in almost every after-school meeting, professional development workshop, or conference I've ever run.

1. **Meditate first.** This might be tricky if the participants have little to no experience with meditation, but if it's at all possible I strongly recommend opening with a small meditation, even if it means including a longer or deeper meditation later in the workshop. An opening meditation clears the room, as well as the mind, and it brings participants more fully into the work.

2. **Use text.** Especially when working with content-focused teachers, an article or short written piece is a great way to frame the discussion. After the opening meditation I always pass out a piece for participants to read. This creates another moment of collective silence and puts everyone on the same page.

3. **Build around a theme.** Find a theme on which to base the meditation, the reading, and the conversation. Teacher meetings can sometimes become extra challenging when the conversation devolves into an airing of grievances or school concerns. This can be avoided by identifying a theme, like space, voice, happiness, or empathy, and making it a central part of the conversation. Having a theme also provides a focus to return to when the conversation does go astray.

4. **Provide space for conversation.** The older the participants, the more space and time for silence they need. They have a lifetime of thoughts swirling around in their heads, and extra time to meditate, to become fully present in the class, or to share their thoughts is important.

5. **Less is more.** Keep it simple. Take the opportunity to prepare for your workshop ahead of time, and then be ready to get through about half of what you set out to do. Think of the readings and prompts as potential guideposts and destinations, being wary of cutting short a meaningful conversation or meditation just to get to the next task. This is a mistake that can be easily made with students as well.

6. **Establish class norms.** I never mention meditation in the first weeks of class; it's only after presenting and establishing a serious tone that I even consider introducing this practice.

CONCLUSION

As the facilitator of a meditation you are tasked with holding a space, a very sacred space for your students and the subconscious mind. Meditation should never be used to fill holes in the curriculum or gaps at the end of a lesson. I find that the most successful meditations come after a rigorous unit or set of tasks is completed. Academics must always precede the practice of meditation, especially when one first introduces it to the class. Members of the administration and parents alike will be reluctant to allow this work in the classroom if they feel it is taking away from learning instead of enriching it. But when meditation is balanced with a rigorous academic experience, the outcome is far beyond what either could offer alone.

GRATITUDE EXERCISE FOR TEACHERS

This activity is recommended for the start of the year, maybe at the first faculty meeting or conference day.

1. Take a minute now and think about the things in your life that give you the greatest joy. Make a list of three items in your life that you love, from the most mundane to the most extraordinary.

2. Now, what about your classroom? Take a moment to write down three more things, this time related to what you enjoy most about teaching.

3. Take three breaths, drop into your heart center, and consider from a deeper level the three aspects of your self that you would be most excited to bring forth into your room, your teaching, and your students' lives this year. Write down that list on the same sheet of paper.

4. Let these three intentions reframe and remind you of the underlying forces at work in your life.

5. Keep this list in your wallet or your notebook, or tape it to your desk. When you find yourself particularly frustrated, whether by a class or an aspect of the school day, look back at the list. Let these nine joys be like a constellation of nine stars that offer direction and add purpose to your work.

ALTERNATE NOSTRIL BREATHING

Find a comfortable spot on a chair or a cushion. Take your dominant hand and fold your three middle fingers into your palm leaving your thumb and pinkie open. Now bring your hand up to your nose, with your thumb to one side and your pinkie to the other. Close your eyes, take three breaths, and begin.

Find some ease in your breath, letting the exhale match your inhale. When you find yourself relaxing, make sure you are breathing through your nose.

Take your thumb (if you are right dominant) or your pinkie (if you are left dominant) and close your right nostril.

Take a few breaths with just the left nostril.

Now rotate to the other side, using the opposite finger to close your left nostril.

Take a few more breaths, using just the right nostril.

Now begin to rotate between inhale and exhale: on the next breath, inhale with the right nostril, but this time switch fingers and exhale through the left nostril. And then on your next breath, breathe in through your left nostril and out the right. Repeat this several times, relaxing through any anxiety that might be bubbling up.

Finally, when you are ready, release your hand and breathe through both nostrils. What do you notice? How has your breath changed? How does your mind feel?

From this exercise you can open your eyes and end the meditation, or use this alternate nostril breathing as the start of a much longer and deeper meditation.

CHAPTER TWELVE

◈◈◈

THE CURRICULUM AND THE COMMUNITY

The success of this work and its impact on students is connected to both how these concepts and practices of meditation are integrated into the core curriculum and also the extent to which the broader community, particularly the parents, buy into the need for greater reflection and more practical tools to deal with stress for their kids. Both the integration of these concepts and practices into the curriculum and the support of the parent community are crucial to the long-term success and sustainability of any meditation initiative.

A NEW CLASS AND A NEW WAY OF TEACHING

A teacher's career journey can sometimes seem to go in circles or spirals, as year after year we repeat the same classes and find ourselves with a new group of students. However, every once in a while we might find ourselves stumbling onto a path outside of those circles and into a class or position we never expected. For me it all started with the Humanities Research Seminar.

In 2012 the principal of my high school approached me with an opportunity. The school, located in a small suburb of New York City, had been asked by the neighboring college to partner in developing a new class. The class was part of an effort to create partnerships between the college and the high school, and at this point it didn't have a name, a syllabus, or even a focus. I had been teaching part-time at the high school for two years while finishing up my graduate coursework. My wife had just been accepted into a full-time doctoral program and would be taking a leave from her own teaching job. I knew that for our financial well-being I needed to try and convince the school to have me on full-time. So when the principal asked me if I was interested in starting this new course, I instantly responded, "Of course." Little did I realize what the creation of this course, the Humanities Research Seminar, would mean for my career or the way I approached teaching.

Several years have now passed, and the class enrollment continues to grow. The Humanities Research Seminar has been the sandbox in which I have developed and nurtured my classroom meditation practice. It has become a safe place where I can veer outside the norms of the curriculum to try new ideas and explorations. It is from this experience that I have developed the five steps of reflection below. Just as you should encourage your students to explore meditation from a safe place, I would also encourage you to find a safe course where you can try it out first before using it across your whole curriculum.

The Five Steps of Reflection: STARS

1. **Space.** First, set up the space. Make sure it is conducive to reflection.
2. **Timing.** Time your reflection as deliberately as you would any activity.
3. **Attention.** Direct the students' attention with a meditation.
4. **Reflection.** Give students an opportunity to reflect alone, often in writing.
5. **Share.** Make space and time so they can share it with the whole group.

I have gone on to use this format in every class I teach and in every meditation workshop I offer. It serves to create the space, the experience, and the window by which to fully integrate and transform memorization into integration, as well as knowledge into wisdom.

BEYOND MINDFULNESS

Recently the high school's director of curriculum and instruction asked me if I'd be interested in offering an online course connected to mindfulness. The school district is part of a regional consortium of schools that contribute, via an online platform, a set courses that would otherwise not be offered in a traditional brick-and-mortar classroom, including courses like Anthropology, Writing a Novella, and Sports Management. The director asked if I'd develop a course, and I came back with a course titled Beyond Mindfulness.

The title was inspired by my desire to introduce students to the roots of meditation and contemplation in both Eastern and Western contexts while also guiding them in applying these ideas to their own lives. The class was to run for eighteen weeks and touch on a number of weekly topics, from foundational Buddhist beliefs to the science of mindfulness and the brain. However, the backbone of the work was to be a series of weekly meditations and a concluding service project, where students took a concept they learned in the class and shared it with a larger audience.

It wasn't until the eighth week of the course that I decided to take a major risk and ask the students to create their own guided meditations, to be shared with the class. Then things really went to the next level. So much of my teaching success is about making intuitive adjustments, and when I think about my own meditative practice, I realize that doing this has connected me to my own intuition. I've become more responsive to those feelings and also a better teacher. I honestly wasn't sure what to expect from these students because I provided minimal guidance beyond the example of the meditations I'd led at the start of the course. What happened next blew me away and changed the whole tenor of the class.

STUDENT-CREATED SCRIPTS FOR GUIDED MEDITATION

I first had each student share the drafts of their script with me, and after revision they shared it on YouTube with the whole class. The students' creativity was beyond my imagination, with meditations on everything from dolphins to removing obstacles on one's path. This project completely changed the direction of the class. The recorded meditations became the backbone of the last ten weeks, inspiring a depth of reflection I couldn't have foreseen when I first made the assignment. Students have such a clear idea of what they need and how to best address that need. Offering them opportunities for authorship empowers them for the rest of their lives. Great teaching redirects the focus back to the student.

The course had started off simply, as students read articles, commented in class forums on one another's posts, and participated in a weekly meditation to develop a personal practice. By the course end, students had shared their growth and reflections with me in a journal and put them together in a final written piece. Here are some excerpts from these end-of-course write-ups.

STUDENT REFLECTIONS

While this class taught me physical lessons such as how to become more skilled at meditation, it has made an even larger impact on my mental self and how I go through life every day. If I am being honest, I am a very happy person overall but there are definitely times when I would consider myself a very anxious person. I get stressed about small things, and tend to overthink decisions I make. It would be an understatement to say this class has helped me drop anxiety and stress. I now feel much more calm and at peace overall.

Jacklyn
June 2018

I always thought I was decent at paying attention to other people and empathizing and sympathizing. This course taught me how to actively pay attention to others and actively pay attention to myself. I learned that it's more than what you say that matters, it's what you do that matters too.

I am also amazed at how talented my classmates were with their own meditations. They must have learned as much as I did in this course because their meditations were good — they worked.

Alice
June 2018

When I first started meditating, I was very hesitant. I was scared of the vulnerable state meditation puts one in, and being in a room with 20 classmates of mine in a vulnerable state wasn't exactly my cup of tea. That might be because I'm very self-conscious, or maybe because I was just scared to put myself out there and try something new. But eventually, I closed my eyes, I dropped into a deeper space, and I found myself.

As I continued to meditate, I began to realize a pattern, and furthermore a parallel. I didn't meditate because I had to for homework anymore; I meditated for a stress-relieving self connection that my inter-being craved, for a mindfulness that I couldn't touch unless I was in a meditative state. And I soon realized, meditation wasn't the only place where I was actively eliminating stress; I was doing it in my daily life un-knowingly as well.

Holly
May 2018

These reflections speak to a deeper desire within students for tools to help them deal with growing stress and anxiety and also for the space to make sense of their changing identities. The guided meditations and the student-led meditations be-came the backbone of the course, and many participants left with a personal practice to support them throughout the rest of high school. Although this particular online course existed outside of the brick-and-mortar structure of the physical building, the foundational components and rituals of reflection we established should be made available to all students.

THE IMPORTANCE OF PARENTAL BUY-IN

If students are at the heart of the classroom, parents are at the heart of the community. Few successful classroom initiatives gain lasting traction without the support of the parents. This is true with issues ranging from reading curriculums to field trips, so it's no surprise that it applies to meditation as well. Like any initiative, a meditation program needs the full support of the community to work. Just as it is important to engage teachers and staff in this process, so too should we connect with parents.

Parents are much like their sons and daughters. I have found that parents will support with unbounded energy those programs that enhance the wellness and growth of their children. However, with the same force that they can use to bring an idea to life, parents will crush any idea if they feel it hurts or hinders their children's learning. I have been incredibly fortunate to have found a highly supportive community around meditation, and I think this is an outgrowth of two things: the ever-growing proliferation of the language surrounding mindfulness in popular culture and the ever-increasing levels of stress present in the lives of young people. These two forces have completely transformed the landscape of meditation in school.

If contextualized appropriately and tied directly to a classroom task, meditation will usually find a receptive audience. This is not to say that there aren't still pockets of resistance to meditation and even mindfulness, especially when these are viewed as an Eastern religious practice. If a group of parents mobilize in opposition to this work, then the chances of implementing these practices or tools in your classroom are very slim; in the most serious circumstances, such a conflict could jeopardize one's teaching career. I would never suggest advocating for a meditation program against parental opposition, nor would I want to encourage anything that would risk someone's job. Thus what I want to share next are techniques and strategies for alleviating parental anxiety around meditation.

Dealing with Parents

- **Be honest.** It is better that you explain your goals and objectives to parents directly rather than through their sons and daughters. Use Back to School Nights and other introductory meetings as opportunities to assure parents that your intention is always to find the best way to support their children, and that meditation is one way to do this.
- **Back it up with data.** While finding scholarly articles on the topic was once challenging, today they are everywhere. When discussing this work, a simple newspaper piece or magazine story might be all you need to open the door. To find something that will work for your community of parents, start with the Garrison Institute website or the studies listed in the bibliography of this book.
- **Check with the administration.** Before reaching out to parents, be sure your administration is on the same page. Just as you would explain to parents the purpose of this work, you need to do the same with the administration. Unfortunately, many school

leaders will be wondering how much work your initiative will create for them, so keep it simple. Explain to them a simple set of objectives and how you'll use these ideas to alleviate the growing anxiety crisis in the school.

- **Start at home.** Reaching out to a core group of parents about starting a meditation circle at one of their homes can be a great way to dispel any unwarranted concerns.

THURSDAY NIGHTS

You can bring meditation directly to the parents. In many cases, they need it just as much as their children do. For me this direct connection developed organically out of my work with students. It was my second year of offering meditation in the classroom when a parent asked me about holding a meditation circle some evening. I was open to the idea, and we went back and forth on a date. Finally, we chose a Thursday at the end of October. The parent agreed to host the circle at her house, and we began.

That first Thursday, we had fifteen participants, all parents of students I taught. Not exactly sure what I'd do with a full hour, I decided to break the evening into three meditations. The first was an extended body scan; the second, a visualization; and the third, an intention setting. After each meditation I opened the circle to sharing.

Fast-Forward

Fast-forward to four years later: the meditation circle now meets every Thursday night. We run it from October to May and continue to host it at a parent's house. The circle has grown in so many ways, guiding the group through loss, grief, challenges, celebrations, and seasons. Whenever I wonder how I'll come up with a new meditation for the evening or wonder if the group has run its course, it always gets deeper and moves to another level. Below is a testimonial from the parent who first invited me to start the group, a foundational member and host.

> As any parent knows, the teenage years are some of the most stressful for a parent. Although not always on a conscious level, I longed to reduce my stress level as a stay-at-home mom. Moreover, I knew instinctively that I should be enjoying my family while we were still together under one roof, and felt I needed to be "living in the moment" more. When the new high school principal came to a welcome lunch at a parent's house, I asked her if she thought Bill would have any interest in guiding a meditation group for parents. She reacted very positively and suggested I contact him. The rest is history! Since then, we have consistently met on Thursday nights during the school year. We have a core group who have been attending since the beginning. We have also had a certain amount of fluidity in the group...as one drops out, others join. Some of our keenest members have joined in the last two years. Our circle has become a powerful resource in our lives, and I'm grateful every day that we have each other.

As I reflect on this experience, I realize that parents are struggling with some of the same issues as their kids — they are overburdened, overscheduled, and overstressed. Meditation, particularly our opening body scan, becomes a way to ground and reorient, to get parents out of their heads and connected once again with the body. In many ways I believe the meditation circle has become the heart of the community. The peace and well-being of the group ripple out across the town. Meditation has become a way to cope with the challenges of parenting, whether it is the diagnosis of an illness or the loss of a friend. The circle lets us know we are not alone.

Tips for Meditating with Parents

1. **Try to find space in a home.** When working with parents, try to find someone who will offer a space in their home. Or find volunteers willing to rotate the hosting.

2. **Keep the groups larger than six but no bigger than fifteen.** This is true for teachers as well as parents. I have found that adults need even more space and opportunity to share their experiences than students. This need becomes problematic when the groups are too big. On the other hand, when groups are too small, you end up with dead time. That's why we run our meditations only when at least six members are present.

3. **Use circles.** When creating the shape for the meditation, I find that sitting in chairs in a circle works best.

4. **Start with a body scan.** I often find that adults and older students need extra time to drop into their bodies at the start of a meditation. They spend a great deal of time in their heads and benefit from a longer opening meditation.

5. **Structure the experience around three meditations.** I begin with a grounding and body scan meditation, follow this with a visualization meditation, and end with an intention meditation.

6. **Connect with the participants' experiences and stresses.** Many adults are parenting two generations, one younger and one older. Trying to honor this unique pressure, as well as helping them find time for self-care, is a big part of the work.

7. **Introduce meditations that tap into the past.** Adults in particular engage with meditations that recall childhood memories. These can also be great tools for remembering lost gifts, as well as forgotten talents and passions.

8. **Give extra time for sharing.** Adults not only need extra time to drop into the meditation, but they also need a little more time to process it as well. Sitting with silence and creating the space for extended reflection can allow everyone to participate and make sense of their experiences.

CONCLUSION

As the work of meditation grows, it has the potential to take on a life of its own. The benefits it can provide for students, teachers, and the broader community are hard to quantify. I can't count the number of times I've now been stopped in the hallway or received a random email from someone in the community who talks about the ways in which a single classroom meditation experience sparked a larger exploration of a topic or theme within their life. I've had secretaries in the school explain how some of my recorded meditations have helped them through struggles with anxiety and sleeplessness. I've heard classroom aides share stories of how sitting in the room as an observer of the practice gave them space to work through the grief of losing a loved one. And I've received emails from students, now in college, sharing stories about integrating meditation into their extracurricular experiences and studies abroad.

The roots of meditation can grow deep and fast. But just as I would warn a teacher not to rush a student in their reflection, it is important to not rush the expansive potential these practices can have on the whole school. Go slow. Start small. You will be amazed at where this will lead.

THE VORTEX MEDITATION

Find a comfortable spot on a chair or cushion. Do not cross your arms or your legs. It's best if you place your hands softly on your legs, or wherever may be most comfortable. Lower your eyes and stare with a soft gaze at the floor or, if you are comfortable doing so, close your eyes.

When you are ready, take three breaths and begin.

Begin to settle into your breath, with each inhale dropping in a little deeper, with each exhale letting go a little more.

Let go of all the sounds around you. If you get distracted, come back to the sound of my voice and your breath.

Feel that firm connection with your seat, the ground, and the earth.

Take a deep, full breath and feel it move down your spine, like a beautiful spiral.

Turn your eyes inward, and see yourself on a beautiful mountain. Imagine yourself among the rocks, the animals, and the birds.

The sun is just coming up over the horizon. A stillness moves across the sky and through your mind.

Breathe in the balance between the sun and the moon, the connections between the stars and the earth.

Breathe in the rocks and the sound of the birds.

Let your whole body release and relax.

All the things you need to do or should do, leave

those down at the bottom of the mountain. Just breathe in space.

Let yourself go even deeper with the breath, into your heart. Feel your heart beating a beautiful rhythm.

Let all the space and the sound fill your heart. Feel your heart open like a flower in the sun.

Let your thoughts be expansive.

With each breath feel a deeper sense of peace move through you, a peace you might feel watching a bird take flight, or a cloud float by, or a stream meandering through the forest.

Let that peace move through your body and out into your life. See that peace spreading to your friendships, your family, and your future.

Feel that breath spiraling down and up, up and down.

And then, and only then, take three long breaths, focusing on the exhale, and when you reach the final one, open your eyes.

CONCLUSION

༄✿ ༄✿ ༄✿

THE INTERIOR

The same medieval period that brought us Chartres Cathedral, the Bohemian alchemists of Prague, and the original contemplative ideas that were later translated and shared by Thomas Merton and Thich Nhat Hanh was a world deeply connected to the stars. The Camino de Santiago, which is located under the Milky Way, was called the Field of Stars. The men and women of that time stared at the night sky, and like their ancestors they told stories of these stars, these burning embers — stories of great gods, brave warriors, and cunning mistresses. In my opinion, the modern world has lost its connection to the stars, and this is part of the reason that the modern classroom has lost the ability to connect students back to themselves.

HUBBLE

An astronomer first broached the concept for the Hubble Telescope in 1923. It was a simple but revolutionary idea. If you could get outside the atmospheric distortion of the earth, incredible views of space and the cosmos awaited. By 1994, that dream became a reality, as the Hubble began beaming back to Earth some of the most breathtaking images ever seen: butterfly nebulae, pillars of creation, supernovas, and even black holes.

A few years after this first wave of photographs arrived, a small group of scientists had an odd idea. They wanted to point the power of Hubble at a part of the night sky where there appeared to be nothing, the deep field. This was a very risky proposition. Almost every minute of the Hubble's time in space, from its launch to its impending decommissioning, had been accounted for, and the idea of wasting precious time and money on nothing went against many top scientists' best judgment.

However, this group persisted. They convinced NASA to point the Hubble at this empty part of space for ten days. At the end of those ten days, what they found was nothing short of earth shattering. The photograph didn't just reveal a few stars; the scientists had literally discovered hundreds of galaxies, some of which defied the very laws of physics in their size and mass.

DEEP FIELD

Today, modern science has shown that you and I contain the very same atoms and molecules that make up the stars. And even more than the elements, we contain the creative potential of the stars within ourselves, through our free will. What we offer students in our schools is just a sliver of the potential that resides in the depths of their heart and being. Teachers should think about their impact and their students' potential in terms of the breadth of the night sky. Like that deep field image painted by the Hubble, this potential may be unknown at first, but it's guaranteed to be earth shattering.

The exploration of the interior life of students has been called many things, from *emotional development* to *spiritual intelligence*. The shifting labeling and ever-changing definitions of what often are the same things make it difficult to coherently capture a clear understanding of this field. However, there is a clear consensus that the inner life of students is greatly neglected in the classroom. Holding a safe and nurturing environment for your classes is a gift, and for some students it might be the only safe space they have.

FULL CIRCLE

Since that first meeting with Zahn Boh, my interest in meditation has grown in leaps and bounds. Soon after our trip to the Zen Center of Detroit, my uncle shared with me a book titled *Living Buddha, Living Christ*,[1] introducing me to Thich Nhat Hanh, and soon after that, Thomas Merton with the work *Thoughts in Solitude*.[2] Thich Nhat Hanh inspired me to see meditation as an active practice that encourages and demands engagement with the world, not separation or isolation. Merton taught me that silence and solitude are the foundations of a balanced and meaningful life.

I share these stories not just to speak of my entry into meditation but also to shed light on the ways in which experiences we have early in our lives can prove formative and directional. Students today, no matter how young, are being exposed to countless ideas and possibilities in school. We must be mindful about the way our own life speaks to them, both consciously and unconsciously. Our presence has a voice far louder than any score or grade. It is our own personal practice of meditation that allows us to give that voice intentionality and power.

We must not forget that it is in our stillness that we find our selves, we find our dreams, and we find our light. And while ignoring the voices of others isn't the answer, failing to hear your own voice in your heart is a crime. Meditation is not a passive or a solitary act; it is an opportunity to explore the inner worlds of your being. Establishing a practice and watching it begin to reframe your whole life and your teaching is where the magic truly resides. What will most surprise you is not that you will find yourself shifting inward, but rather that you will begin to shift outward and engage more fully with the world around you, both as a human being and as a teacher.

THE DOORWAY MEDITATION

Before starting the meditation, ask students to write down three questions related to their topic or research interest.

Find a comfortable seat on a cushion or chair. Turn your gaze downward or, if you are comfortable doing so, close your eyes completely. When you are ready, take three breaths and begin.

Follow your breath and attention into your heart center.

Imagine a place and space where you feel completely comfortable, totally safe, and where you are your fullest self.

As you breathe in, let yourself explore this space. What do you feel? What do you see? What do you remember?

As you take this next breath, picture yourself turning around in a full circle, taking in everything around you.

As you come back facing forward, picture a door in front of you. It can be floating in the air or part of a structure — whatever feels most comfortable to you.

As you walk closer, you can feel that this is a special door, a magical one connected to your questions. Reach out and touch the door. Notice the material, the shape, the feel, even the smell.

When you are ready, you are going to step through this door. On the other side you'll find something unexpected, unimaginable.

Take a deep breath, and open the door.

Take another, and step over the threshold into a vast empty space.

Take a third breath, and feel your feet land on hard ground.

Turn your attention to your feet. What are you standing on? Grass, rocks, a road, a floor? Are you wearing anything on your feet? Or are you barefoot?

Now, slowly shift your attention upward, to your ankles, then your wrists, and even your hair. What are you wearing? Bracelets, a robe, a suit of armor?

Look at your surroundings. Where are you? A city, a forest, alone, in a crowd? Is it night or day, cloudy or sunny? Is there happiness around you, or fear?

Turn your attention inward, and recall your first question. As you say it in your mind, feel yourself effortlessly taken to a place, a person, or a thing that can offer an answer.

Open yourself fully to the answer. Maybe it is a word, a thought, or an image. Don't judge, just listen. No expectations, no control — just breathe.

When you feel satisfied, take another deep breath and recall your second question. Effortlessly let yourself be drawn to the answer. No judgment, no control — just let whatever comes, come. Sit with that answer, don't rush it. Let it unfold naturally and organically however it chooses.

Now when you are ready, ask your third question. What comes to mind? An answer, a further question, an image? Just let this flow naturally and effortlessly, as you have before. Feel yourself *in* the answer, not just observing it.

Step back and breathe in all you have learned.

Then take a deep sigh, and breathe all of it out.

Feel a sense of gratitude fill your heart for all you have discovered and learned. If you would like, make an offering to this space. Place it on the ground before you.

Then as you take your next breath, see the world and images around you dissolving.

Take a deep breath and step back through the doorway.

And then finally, when you are ready, take your final breath and reenter your body.

FREQUENTLY ASKED QUESTIONS

How long should a meditation be?

It depends. I've led meditations as short as a single minute and as long as forty minutes. However, most meditations I lead are between twelve and fifteen minutes long. This seems to be the perfect length of time to get students to settle into their bodies and connect with the inner landscape of their minds.

What if a parent doesn't want their child meditating in my classroom?

Because honoring both the parents' wishes and the students' desires is first and foremost, I recommend first getting parent permission, particularly for younger kids, before introducing the practice. I always frame meditation as an invitation and a powerful reflective practice. If parents still object, you can replace meditation with quiet journaling or reading; these can have a similar effect on a classroom.

What should I do if a meditation upsets a student?

This will sometimes happen when you use meditation to explore the inner landscape of the heart. If you look around the room after the meditation, you can get a pretty quick and accurate read of the emotional experience on most students' faces. As we go around the circle, sharing, I always remind students that they can pass and are never obligated to share. If it appears to me that a student is upset, I usually follow up with them immediately after class. If the issue seems serious, I escort them directly to their guidance counselor and call home.

I have never meditated with my class before. How would you recommend starting?

If this is your first meditation, start before an assignment or a test with some easily accessible imagery (nature, a flower, the ocean, a candle). A simple breathing exercise in these moments of anxiety can have an instant impact and begin to reinforce the benefits of meditation to the students.

Do you have any recommendations about what I should *never* do in a meditation?

- Never rush a meditation. If you feel rushed, save it for another day.
- Never use meditation to fill time in your class. A good meditation is as well timed and thought out as a great lesson.
- Never be evaluative in a meditation. Students are constantly getting feedback on their actions and words. Try to refrain from this kind of language and honor what students choose to share or not share.

What time of year is best for meditating?

I have found that there are several times a year that work best. Right before a holiday break, such as Thanksgiving or winter break, can be an ideal time for reflection. Students often feel settled into the class by this point in the year, and meditation can be a great way of exploring where they've been and where they would like to go. Another great time is the spring or the end of year; this is the perfect space for lengthier reflection. If a meditation practice is well established in the classroom by this point, going outside can help make the meditation feel special. However, as you feel more comfortable in your practice and in leading students in their practice, you'll discover that you know the time best for meditation.

I'm struggling with a lot of outside noise in my building, which makes meditation almost impossible. Any suggestions?

This is a real challenge in schools because much of the noise in the building is outside of our control. First, try to time your meditations during a period or block that is quieter. Maybe meditating in the middle of class is better than meditating at the start or finish. Also consider putting a sign outside the door: "Quiet. Meditation in Progress." Lastly, if you have access to speakers and a computer, you can find an infinite number of quiet instrumental pieces on YouTube (search for "yoga music") to play in the background. This can create a white noise that drowns out the other sounds.

What if students start laughing when I begin the meditation?

They will, especially if they are new to the practice, so don't be surprised. Taking a deep breath and closing your eyes is a very unsettling feeling for most students in a classroom environment; actually, it probably is unsettling in any environment. When this happens I just continue with the meditation. I don't pretend the laughter doesn't exist — I just don't honor it. Honestly though, this is more of an issue with students who aren't familiar with the norms of your classroom than with those who are.

What should I do if a student's phone goes off or a student arrives late to class?

Keep meditating. Most students will find a seat on their own, and most phone calls eventually come to an end. It is usually a good idea to remind students to turn their phones off before you start.

How do I deepen my own meditation practice?

Be gentle and realistic with your practice. Don't set an expectation for your practice that is unrealistic or impossible to meet. It is better to meditate four to six minutes every day than twenty minutes two or three times a week. Also, make the weekends special. I sometimes move my meditations from the morning to the evening on the weekends, and I usually take a break on Friday and Saturday.

Is there a specific position you would recommend for meditation?

I find that sitting on chairs is usually the most comfortable and effective body position when working with students. Obviously, as students become more comfortable with the practice you might have them sit crossed-legged on the floor or even let them lie down on a yoga mat, but for beginning meditations I would recommend just simply sitting on a chair. The other caveat I would make is that when students are seated and preparing for a meditation, nothing should be crossed — no crossed arms or crossed legs. While I might have my thumbs touch when I meditate alone at home, I find that in a group meditation, especially in a circle, being more physically open allows everyone to benefit from the collective energy. As the meditation deepens, I sometimes find myself gently rocking back and forth to the rhythm of the words.

How do you transition a class into a meditation?

I always start by having everyone move their desks to the outside of the room and then arrange the chairs in a circle in the middle. I then have the students write down a simple intention for the meditation in their notebook before placing it under their chair. I ask the students to uncross their arms and legs, place their hands on their thighs, and focus their eyes on a spot on the floor three or four feet in front of them. And then I begin.

What kind of visuals do you use when guiding students in a meditation?

You name it, I've done it and used it. Kids are incredibly open, and their imaginations are amazing. If I am just starting out with a group, I usually have them breathe for the first minute, just observing their breath and body. Then I encourage them to release any thoughts, like balloons into the sky, and then I invite them to look into their hearts. Sometimes just this simple meditation can lead to a powerful class discussion.

Is everyone required to share?

Require is a dangerous word when it comes to meditation. Everything is an invitation. Usually I just start going around the circle and look at each student. Most kids are excited to share, and this has a domino effect on everyone else.

Do you have them share out immediately after?

No. I always give the class a few minutes to write down or draw what they saw or felt. To me this is just as important as the meditation itself.

Do you script what you are going to say?

No. I never script anything. I have an idea, but not a script. I try to remain in the natural flow of the meditation.

Do you close your eyes?

I've led meditations both ways, but I find that having my eyes closed is better. You really need to be out of the visual space and into your mind's eye to avoid distractions. But be authentic. Students can always sense when you are not being real with them or are not comfortable.

Has anything unexpected ever happened from a meditation?

One of the unexpected outcomes of guided meditations is the ability to create a sense of empathy and compassion within students. I have seen this occur when meditations lead the student to engage with friends and family in their own lives, and I've also seen this take place when they connect with historical figures from a thousand or two thousand years ago.

Do you have any final advice for someone who has never led a meditation before?

Trust your instincts. Leading a meditation is different than actually meditating because in many ways you are holding the space for the group, not participating fully in it. Try to stay relaxed and keep returning to the breath.

APPENDIX OF ACTIVITIES AND MEDITATIONS

THE MANDALA ACTIVITY

Background

Located at the end of the North Transept in Chartres Cathedral is a large stained-glass window. In the Gothic tradition, this specific type of stained-glass installation is known as a Rose Window. Characterized by a circular shape, central figure, and radial design, the Rose Window is highly prominent in the Gothic cathedrals of medieval Europe. This particular Rose Window in Chartres Cathedral features as its central design Jesus, sitting in Mary's lap. Surrounding this central figure are four doves, representing the four evangelists. The piece also features angels, disciples, and other biblical characters. Although the content of the Rose Window is strictly Christian, its stylistic form predates the Gospels themselves.

The design of the Rose Window references mandala art of

ancient Eastern religions like Hinduism and Buddhism. In the Hindu tradition, mandalas represented a microcosm of the universe, with a deity in the middle representing the center of the cosmos, and radial, symmetrical patterns around this point. In Buddhist temples, or stupas, the floor plan is based on a mandala. Essentially, this basic design is employed to portray ideas of divinity, inwardness, and interconnectedness.

Directions

Schools have cycles of beginnings, middles, and ends. Each offers an incredible opportunity for meditation. The desire to reflect and take inventory of their experience is always present within young people, and meditation offers the perfect doorway. Offer one of the guided meditations from an earlier chapter. ("Candle Meditation," "Light Meditation," or "Rooting Meditation" work well with this activity.)

Activity

After the meditation, using paper plates, have the students create mandalas that represent their own lives, with themselves as the central figure. The plate can be divided into four or eight sections. Each piece can represent a specific aspect, talent, connection, or wish (collect these afterward for future use).

- Where do they see interconnectedness?
- What cycles appear in their lives?
- Who and what do they choose to surround themselves with?

Conclude with a discussion about the circular nature of life and the school year. Invite students to visualize their lives as mandalas going forward.

Materials

- Paper plates
- Markers and crayons
- Rulers

COLLEGE ADMISSION ESSAY

This meditation is designed to facilitate deeper student reflection on their college admission essays. This can be an especially difficult task for many high school students because it is the first time they have been asked to reflect on their life, and the stakes feel so high. Here you'll find a guided meditation, guiding questions and tips to offer the students, and suggestions for leading this experience. If this is being led by a guidance counselor or teacher in a large group, it might be useful to put students into smaller groups after the meditation so that they can more freely share their thoughts.

Materials

- Notebooks or paper to write on
- Pencils or markers

Guiding Questions

- How do you define learning?
- When have you experienced genuine learning in your life?
- Who or what has been your greatest teacher?

Tips for Writing Your Essay

- Contrast brings clarity. Look for the contrast in your stories and meditations.
- Try to engage two to three senses in your opening to draw the reader into the story.
- Show, don't tell. In your essay try to show a feeling, rather than telling it to the reader.

- Don't give away the ending until the actual end. If your essay builds suspense, save the resolution until the final paragraph.
- Consider structuring the essay in three parts.
  - First is the action, dropping the reader into an exciting moment of the story.
  - The second part is an opportunity to give the backstory and events that led to the story you shared in the first part.
  - The third part of your essay should reflect on the story, why you told it, and how it has changed you. It is always nice to have an ending that also discusses how this experience has shaped you as a person and how it aligns with the future self you envision. This is where you can also mention how the colleges you are applying to support that vision.

Here is a simple meditation that will help students reflect on high school and awaken memories that speak to who they are.

COLLEGE ESSAY MEDITATION

First find a comfortable spot on a chair or cushion. I ask you not to cross your arms or your legs. It's best if you just place your hands softly on your thighs, or wherever may be most comfortable. When you are ready, lower your eyes and just stare with a soft gaze at the floor or the desk or, if you are comfortable doing so, close your eyes. Take three breaths and begin.

Shift your focus away from outside distractions and inward to your breath.

Sit in this space for a few moments, just observing the breath with no judgment, no control, no need to change it. Observe the length, the depth, the balance between the inhale and the exhale.

When you are ready, shift your focus to your thoughts. As with your breath, just observe them. No judgment, no need to change or control them.

Take each of these thoughts and place them to the side of your mind. You can even imagine putting them in little boxes or letting them float away on the ends of balloons.

As your thoughts begin to leave you, turn your attention and focus even further inward.

Follow your breath down into your heart.

How does your heart feel? Is it heavy? Is it light? Do you notice darker spots and places?

With no judgment, just observe.

With this next breath, turn your awareness even further inward, even deeper, and imagine that you are stepping into a room.

It can be any room — your bedroom, a room from your childhood or another house, maybe even a room you've never seen before.

Notice the walls, the space, the shelves. Imagine that this room is filled with things. But not just any things; it's filled with objects connected to you, almost like a museum of your life.

Each object has a memory and a meaning attached to it. See if you can reach out and touch one. What do you feel? What do you notice? What do you remember?

This could go on forever, but when you are ready I want you to shift your attention to a collection of books against the far wall. If there are no shelves, just imagine the books are stacked in a pile.

Walk over to the books. Notice the bindings, the material, and the smell of these books. Some are old and some are new.

Let your eyes be drawn to one of the books. Maybe you notice your name written on the outside.

Imagine yourself wiping the dust off the book, feeling its energy and warmth in your hands. This is a special book — it is the book of your life. When you are ready, but only when you are ready, open this book.

You might find it full of words, you might find it full of images, or maybe you just have feelings as you turn the pages.

When you are ready, I want you to turn to the last three or four chapters of the book, to the end. Imagine that some of these chapters represent a year of your life. Some of the chapters are bigger than others, some might have more words, and some might just have images.

I want you to turn to a moment in this book that holds a very powerful experience you had in the past four years. Maybe it was with a friend, or maybe it was when you were alone.

Notice how the book seems to read your thoughts, and maybe it even turns the pages on its own. Whatever comes to mind, trust it.

Now see if you can find a moment in these pages that speaks to your passions. What have you come to love? What have you grown or nurtured over these past three or four years? Trust what comes to your heart.

Now turn toward the end of the book, the very last page.

On this final page is a single word, a very important word, a word that represents the essence of who you are. If nothing appears, just imagine something. There is no right or wrong word. Trust what you see.

Now see yourself closing this book and returning it to the shelf or the pile. You can come back to it whenever you so choose, but for now let it go.

Take another breath and see yourself leaving this special space.

Take another breath and feel yourself reentering your body.

Take one final breath and see yourself sitting back in your seat.

Post-meditation Instructions

At this point you might have students get out crayons or markers to draw their experience as well as write it. The act of using childhood tools can awaken even more memories.

You might also have the students begin to draw a web of words and images around the final word in the meditation, their essence. Let them take as much time as they need. This is what I call "heart-storming," and it can be a great tool for facilitating creative reflection. Don't rush them during this activity. Combining this meditation with the mandala exercise described in the appendix can also be a great way to open their imaginations.

THE EARTH MEDITATION
(ALTERNATE ROOTING MEDITATION)

First find a comfortable spot on a chair or cushion. I ask you not to cross your arms or your legs. It's best if you just place your hands softly on your thighs, or wherever may be most comfortable. I ask you to lower your eyes and just stare with a soft gaze at the floor or the desk or, if you are comfortable doing so, close your eyes. Take three breaths and begin.

With each breath, find yourself moving further and further into your body, until you reach your heart center.

Take a moment to check in with your heart at this moment. How does it feel? How does it sound? What may be residing there?

Then, when you are ready, I want you to take another deep breath and shift your awareness all the way down to the bottom of your feet. See if you can find that point of connection between your body and the ground.

Take another breath, and see if you can imagine that point of connection dissolving and a set of roots growing out of your feet and into the ground.

Take another breath, and feel those roots beginning to move through the floor, into the soft soil of the earth, and then even deeper into the bedrock. Feel yourself rooted into the earth.

Then, with this next breath I want you to take all of the anxiety, all of the fear, all of the doubt you might have felt in your heart earlier, and release it into the earth. Let go of all the concerns and cares that you've carried with you through the day and the week. Feel them run down your spine and legs, like water into a pool.

With each breath, more and more of those fears pass through your body and into the earth.

Now on this next breath, I want you to imagine a new energy from the earth moving up through the roots of the ground and into your legs. Give this new energy and warmth a color. Feel it begin to fill your legs and move up your spine and into your chest. Take another breath and feel it fill your head.

This new energy is light, clear, and warm.

Feel this new energy create a lightness in your mind or a tingling sensation in your fingers.

Take another breath and feel it fill your lungs.

Let this light fill your chest and begin to expand around your heart center as if it were a balloon.

Take another deep breath and feel it fill your lungs. Let this light fill your chest and begin to expand around your whole body, as if you were in a cocoon of light and color.

Take another deep breath, and feel the stillness of this space and place that surrounds you. The warmth and healing of this new energy is moving through your mind, your thoughts, your intentions. Feel the joy and abundance that spring from the depths of your heart now radiating through your whole body.

Now take three more breaths. With each breath, the light will begin to shrink, this time almost like a balloon deflating. The light will get smaller and smaller until it's a dense orb of light at the center of your heart.

Now you will carry this light with you for the rest of the day and into the evening. Everyone you meet will see this light in your eyes and feel it in your heart.

When you are ready, and only then, take three long breaths, focusing on the exhales, and when you reach the final one, open your eyes.

THE LIGHT MEDITATION

Find a comfortable spot on a chair or cushion. First, I ask you not to cross your arms or your legs. It's best if you just place your hands softly on your legs, or wherever may be most comfortable. When you are ready, either lower your eyes and just stare with a soft gaze at the floor or the desk or, if you are comfortable doing so, close your eyes.

Now, I want you to take three breaths and begin. With each breath, I want you to move deeper and deeper into your mind's eye. Let go of any thoughts, worries, or desires you might have.

As you breathe, you find yourself moving deeper and deeper inside of yourself. I want you now to draw your attention away from your mind and any of the distractions of your body, and move it into your heart center.

I want you now to imagine that there is a light at the center of your heart. With each breath you move closer to the light.

Now, as you approach the light you discover that it contains something incredibly special and wondrous, something just for you. Within that light is the talent or love that you enjoy the most in your life — maybe it's a friend's face, or a baby in your arms. Imagine as you move closer and closer to that light that you feel that joy and wonder deep in your own heart.

Now, as you feel that wonder, I want you to take another deep breath. This time as you breathe in, imagine that feeling expanding in your chest. It grows with each breath, almost like a balloon, and now you can feel it filling every part of your being.

With each breath, that light moves into your arms, your legs, your neck, your mind, and you can feel that joy tingling from the tips of your fingers to your little toes.

Now, I want you to imagine moving through the rest of your day. Everyone you see will notice that joy in your eyes. Everyone you touch will feel it in your hands. It will be contagious, passing from you to others, and what is most beautiful is that now you will see the light and joy that resides within them.

Now, take three filling breaths. And as you take these final breaths, I want you to move back into yourself, your body, your mind, but always carrying, always holding that joy that resides at the center of your heart.

At the end of each day, practice this simple meditation. Notice how your light changes, notice how you change. Over time, you will nurture a deeper sense of peace that will accompany you throughout the day. The light of your heart will be visible in your eyes, and you will be able to see more easily the light of other peoples' candles in their eyes. Recognizing the unique light within each person is the first step to spreading compassion throughout the world.

ACKNOWLEDGMENTS

The ideas in this book were first introduced to me almost thirty years ago when I walked into the Detroit Zen Center. If it weren't for my uncle's willingness to open a door for me into a spiritual world I had only read about in books, I might never have started on this incredible path.

Books are made of more than just ideas; they also require a lot of hard work, support, and expertise. I owe my literary agents, Clelia Gore and Adria Goetz, a great debt of gratitude for finding this idea a home. To Jason Gardner, my editor, who took a chance on the proposal, you expressed a great deal of passion and enthusiasm for this work from the moment we first spoke. I'm deeply thankful for your guiding vision. To Patricia Heinicke, an amazing copy editor, who identified the indecipherable parts of the manuscript and brought them back together in a clear and insightful way, I'm so grateful. To my wife, Lauren Meyer, thank you for believing in this idea from the moment I first shared it with you on the trails of Blue Hill at Stone Barns. And to my son, Liam, who keeps me mindfully grounded with his words, his laughter, and his hugs, thank you. I also want to thank all the students who shared their voices and experiences in these pages. Several were named directly in the text, but many who remain unnamed played an equally important role in showing me the full potential of this work. For the parents who have opened their homes to create circles and spaces of reflection, as well as my whole school community, which nurtured opportunities for exploration and introspection, thank you.

And lastly, I'd like to say a special thanks to a group of heroes who played an unexpected role in making this story possible. In the middle of the writing process, I found out I needed open-heart surgery. The experience changed me, but it also changed this book, deepening the words and the expression of what I hoped it would communicate, not just about teaching, but about life. I owe a great deal of gratitude to Dr. Girardi, Dr. Miller, Dr. Jones, and the other amazing professionals at Weill Cornell Medical Center.

It takes a team to write a book and a loving family to heal a heart. I've been lucky to have both. Thank you.

GLOSSARY OF KEY TERMS

Authenticity: Aligning your voice with your actions is the most powerful form of authenticity. Never ask of the students something you don't ask of yourself, and this is also true of meditation. If you don't have a practice, don't expect them to. And if you have never tried a specific meditation, don't experiment on them.

Balance: Meditation is a great tool in helping all members of the community find balance between action and stillness. Both play a role in schools, and neglecting one or the other will lead to problems down the road.

Breath: A silk thread connecting us to the present moment, the breath makes us more aware of our actions and more aware of the loving kindness we share with the world. It is also the foundation of any meditation practice. I recommend always opening meditations with three long breaths and ending meditations with three long breaths. It takes a moment to settle into a meditation, as it also takes a moment to settle back into the physical body at the end. These three slow and rhythmic breaths have the power to do both.

Chakras: The rainbow of energies swirling inside of us is described as the seven chakras. In Hinduism, the chakras are believed to be seven points of energy within our physical bodies. A different color and a different lotus flower represent each chakra. With a simple visualization we can imagine our chakras spinning inside of us, open and balanced.

Distraction: As we enter the day, many distractions take us away from our hearts and fill our minds with thoughts. It is important to pause and catch our breath amidst all the noise and distraction.

Energy: The life force that flows through us is an energy. Some call this energy *prana* or *cosmic energy*. When we focus on our breath, we awaken a deeper energy within ourselves that can carry us through the day with peace and harmony.

Fun: Life is meant to be lived and enjoyed; it is meant to be full of fun. Meditation helps us be more present in the current moment so we may enjoy being with our family, our friends, and our selves.

Grounding: There is no right or wrong way to meditate, as long as you are comfortable. Some people like to meditate seated on a chair, while others cross their legs and sit on the ground. However you are sitting, the act of connecting to the body and grounding with the floor or the earth can bring us more fully into the present. Grounding can place us on a foundation of health and well-being from which we embrace the present moment.

Happiness: When we are connected to our hearts, our passions, and our talents, we are filled with happiness and joy.

Heart: In ancient Egypt, the heart was considered the seat of the soul. In the Hindu chakras, the heart is believed to be the bridge between the physical and the energetic worlds. Cultivating a connection with the heart in meditation can be very powerful. The language of the heart is often expressed through our emotions. A teacher connected to their heart has the ability to connect to the hearts of their students.

The Hero's Journey: This is a powerful set of archetypes and stages one can use when guiding a meditation or reflecting on one's life's journey and work.

Interior: Thomas Merton once said, "Our real journey in life is interior." Meditation is a tool for opening the doorway into this journey.

Intuition: Trust your intuition. It might be telling you something about timing, or about which type of meditation to engage in on a particular day, or it might even be about checking in with a student. Your intuition is one of your greatest resources as a teacher. The more it is used, the greater it grows.

Meditation: The practice of meditation helps us to discover our uniqueness and the hidden truths within our heart. One of those truths is that we are all connected.

Passion: We want to teach with passion, but we also want to connect to the passion within our students. Passion isn't something that comes from the head; it dwells in the heart.

Personal journey: We all have a unique path to walk in this world. Through moments of silence and solitude, we can mindfully choose which direction we will take.

Present moment: Meditation allows us to access the gifts of the present moment and nurture a peace within our hearts so that we may share with others throughout the day.

Questions: Who am I? Why am I here? What is my purpose? Through meditation we often find ourselves asking these universal questions. Find comfort in the questions, and know they are signposts on the path to self-realization.

Reflection: Cultivate silence and moments of alone time, not just in your meditations but also in your classroom. This internal time is for deeper exploration of the self and overall wellness.

Service: The inner work has meaning only if it meets the needs of the outer world. Service is how we share the fruits of our practice with others and the global community.

Silence and solitude: Through moments of silence we can reconnect to the sacred spirit within ourselves and then more easily connect to the spirit within others.

Simplicity: Keep your meditations as simple as possible. Often the simplest meditations are the most powerful for students.

Third eye: The meditator closes their outer eyes to the distractions of the world, and opens the third eye to see the infinite within. Open your third eye, and let your imagination spread like a ripple across the sea of consciousness.

Wholeness: Cultivating wholeness in the classroom is important to developing students who are balanced and well. Wholeness means bringing the self, both the external and the internal, to the learning process.

Wisdom: Each day students have a thousand new experiences. Meditation allows students to internalize these new experiences into knowledge that they hold within their hearts, or wisdom.

NOTES

CHAPTER ONE: HISTORY

1. See, for example, John Dewey, *Human Nature and Conduct* (New York: Henry Holt, 1923).

2. For an example of this latter approach, see Stephen Tomlinson and his exploration of the influence John Dewey and Edward Thorndike had on this modern debate: Stephen Tomlinson, "Edward Lee Thorndike and John Dewey on the Science of Education," *Oxford Review of Education* 23, no. 3 (1997): 365–83.

3. Diane Ravitch dissects Race to the Top in her analysis of the context of corporate reforms in education: Diane Ravitch, *Reign of Error: The Hoax of the Privatization Movement and the Danger to America's Public Schools* (New York: Vintage, 2013).

4. Peter Wood, in his *Drilling through the Core* (Boston: Pioneer Institute for Public Policy Research, 2015), explores the Common Core in depth and critiques the outside donors and players that have shaped these reforms.

5. For more on this, see Tobin Hart, *From Information to Transformation:*

Education for the Evolution of Consciousness (Ann Arbor, MI: Peter Lang, 2001), 135.

6. Hart, *From Information to Transformation.*
7. Smitha Mundasad, "Mindfulness Classes to 'Help Teenagers' Mental Fitness,'" *BBC News*, July 15, 2015, www.bbc.com/news /health-33540242.
8. Lauren Cassini Davis, "When Mindfulness Meets the Classroom," *The Atlantic*, August 31, 2015, www.theatlantic.com/education /archive/2015/08/mindfulness-education-schools-meditation /402469; and Jeanne Chadwick and Nicholas W. Gelbar, "Mindfulness for Children in Public Schools: Current Research and Developmental Issues to Consider," *International Journal of School & Educational Psychology* 4, no. 2 (2016): 106–12.
9. Jeff Q. Bostic et al., "Being Present at School: Implementing Mindfulness in Schools," *Child & Adolescent Psychiatric Clinics* 24, no. 2 (April 2015): 245–59.
10. See Engel v. Vitale, 370 US 421 (1962); Abington School District v. Shempp, 374 US 203 (1963); Lemon v. Kurtzman, 403 US 602 (1971).
11. See Hart, *From Information to Transformation.*
12. Amanda Machado, "Should Schools Teach Kids to Meditate?" *The Atlantic*, January 27, 2014, www.theatlantic.com/education/archive /2014/01/should-schools-teach-kids-to-meditate/283229.

CHAPTER TWO: TOOLS

1. Nirmal Joshi, "Doctor, Shut Up and Listen," *New York Times*, January 4, 2015, www.nytimes.com/2015/01/05/opinion/doctor -shut-up-and-listen.html.

CHAPTER FOUR: SILENCE AND SOLITUDE

1. James Martin, *Becoming Who You Are: Insights on the True Self from Thomas Merton and Other Saints* (Mahwah, NJ: Paulist Press, 2006).

2. *Into Great Silence*, directed by Philip Gröning (US release 2007; originally released in 2005 as *Die grosse Stille*).

3. Christopher Queen and Sallie King, *Engaged Buddhism: Buddhist Liberation Movements in Asia* (Albany, NY: SUNY Press, 1996), 411.

4. Queen and King, *Engaged Buddhism*, 354.

5. Thich Nhat Hanh, *Planting Seeds: Practicing Mindfulness with Children* (Berkeley, CA: Parallax Press, 2011).

6. Thich Nhat Hanh, *Planting Seeds*.

7. Thomas Merton, *Love and Living* (London: Sheldon Press, 1986), 3.

CHAPTER FIVE: THE CLASSROOM

1. Joseph Campbell, *The Hero with a Thousand Faces* (Novato, CA: New World Library, 2008).

2. Parker Palmer, *The Courage to Teach: Exploring the Inner Landscape of a Teacher's Life* (San Francisco, CA: Wiley & Sons, 1998), 166.

CHAPTER SEVEN: HIGH SCHOOL

1. Paulo Coelho, *The Alchemist: 25th Anniversary Edition* (New York: HarperOne, 2014).

2. Paulo Coelho, *The Pilgrimage: A Contemporary Quest for Ancient Wisdom* (London: Thorsons, 2012).

3. Brother David Steindl-Rast, "Want to Be Happy? Be Grateful," filmed June 2013, TED video, 14:27, www.ted.com/talks/david _steindl_rast_want_to_be_happy_be_grateful.

CHAPTER EIGHT: FIELD TRIPS

1. Campbell, *The Hero with a Thousand Faces*, 18.

CHAPTER NINE: TRAGEDY AND TRAUMA

1. David B. Feldman, "Why Daydreaming Is Good for Us," *Psychology Today*, December 19, 2017, www.psychologytoday.com /us/blog/supersurvivors/201712/why-daydreaming-is-good-us.

CHAPTER TEN: ELEMENTARY SCHOOL

1. E. B. White, *Charlotte's Web* (New York: HarperCollins Publishers, 1999).
2. Anne Troy and Phyllis Green, *The Whipping Boy by Sid Fleischman* [teaching guide] (Palatine, IL: A. Troy and P. Green, 1988).

CHAPTER ELEVEN: TEACHERS

1. Thich Nhat Hanh and Katherine Weare, *Happy Teachers Change the World: A Guide for Cultivating Mindfulness in Education* (Berkeley, CA: Parallax Press, 2017).

CONCLUSION: THE INTERIOR

1. Thich Nhat Hanh, *Living Buddha, Living Christ* (New York: Penguin, 1995).
2. Thomas Merton, *Thoughts in Solitude* (New York: Farrar, Straus and Giroux, 2000).

BIBLIOGRAPHY

Bostic, Jeff Q., Michael D. Nevarez, Mona P. Potter, Jefferson B. Prince, Margaret Benningfield, and Blaise A. Aguirre. "Being Present at School." *Child and Adolescent Psychiatric Clinics of North America* 24 (2015): 245–59.

Campbell, Joseph. *The Hero with a Thousand Faces*. Novato, CA: New World Library, 2008.

Chadwick, Jeanne, and Nicholas W. Gelbar. "Mindfulness for Children in Public Schools: Current Research and Developmental Issues to Consider." *International Journal of School & Educational Psychology* 4, no. 2 (2016): 106–12.

Coelho, Paulo. *The Pilgrimage: A Contemporary Quest for Ancient Wisdom*. London: Thorsons, 2012.

Coelho, Paulo. *The Alchemist: 25th Anniversary Edition*. Translated by Alan R. Clarke. New York: HarperOne, 2014.

Davis, Lauren Cassini. "When Mindfulness Meets the Classroom." *The Atlantic*, August 31, 2015. www.theatlantic.com/education/archive /2015/08/mindfulness-education-schools-meditation/402469.

Dewey, John. *Human Nature and Conduct*. New York: Henry Holt, 1923.

Feldman, David. "Why Daydreaming Is Good for Us." *Psychology Today*, December 19, 2017. www.psychologytoday.com/us/blog /supersurvivors/201712/why-daydreaming-is-good-us.

Gröning, Philip. *Into Great Silence*. New York: Zeitgeist Films, 2007 (wide release). Originally released in 2005 as *Die grosse Stille*. Directed by Philip Gröning.

Hanh, Thich Nhat. *Living Buddha, Living Christ*. New York: Penguin, 1995.

———. *Planting Seeds: Practicing Mindfulness with Children*. Berkeley, CA: Parallax Press, 2011.

Hanh, Thich Nhat, and Katherine Weare. *Happy Teachers Change the World: A Guide for Cultivating Mindfulness in Education*. Berkeley, CA: Parallax Press, 2017.

Hart, Tobin. *From Information to Transformation: Education for the Evolution of Consciousness*. Ann Arbor, MI: Peter Lang, 2001.

Iezzi, Teressa. "How Neil deGrasse Tyson Discovered Manhattanhenge." *Fast Company*, May 29, 2015. www.fastcompany.com/3046868/how-neil-degrasse-tyson-discovered-manhattanhenge.

Joshi, Nirmal. "Doctor, Shut Up and Listen." *New York Times*, January 4, 2015. www.nytimes.com/2015/01/05/opinion/doctor-shut-up-and-listen.html.

Machado, Amanda. "Should Schools Teach Kids to Meditate?" *The Atlantic*, January 27, 2014. www.theatlantic.com/education/archive/2014/01/should-schools-teach-kids-to-meditate/283229.

Martin, James. *Becoming Who You Are: Insights on the True Self from Thomas Merton and Other Saints*. Mahwah, NJ: Paulist Press, 2006.

McMurrer, J. *Choices, Changes, and Challenges: Curriculum and Instruction in the NCLB Era*. Center on Education Policy. Washington, DC, 2007.

Merton, Thomas. *Love and Living*. London: Sheldon Press, 1986.

———. *Thoughts in Solitude*. New York: Farrar, Straus and Giroux, 2000.

MindfulCloud PBC. "Oprah Winfrey Talks with Thich Nhat Hanh Excerpt — Powerful." YouTube video, 21:47. Posted May 12, 2013. www.youtube.com/watch?v=NJ9UtuWfs3U.

Mundasad, Smitha. "Mindfulness Classes to 'Help Teenagers' Mental Fitness.'" *BBC News*. July 15, 2015.

Palmer, Parker J. *The Courage to Teach: Exploring the Inner Landscape of a Teacher's Life*. San Francisco: Wiley & Sons, 1998.

Queen, Christopher, and Sallie King. *Engaged Buddhism: Buddhist Liberation Movements in Asia*. Albany, NY: SUNY Press, 1996.

Ravitch, Diane. *Reign of Error: The Hoax of the Privatization Movement and the Danger to America's Public Schools*. New York: Vintage, 2013.

Steindl-Rast, David. "Want to Be Happy? Be Grateful." Video and transcript. Filmed at TEDGlobal 2013. TED video, 14:27. www.ted.com/talks/david_steindl_rast_want_to_be_happy_be_grateful/transcript?language=en.

Tomlinson, S. "Edward Lee Thorndike and John Dewey on the Science of Education." *Oxford Review of Education* 23 (1997): 365–83.

Troy, Anne, and Phyllis Green. *The Whipping Boy by Sid Fleischman [teaching guide]*. Palatine, IL: A. Troy and P. Green, 1988.

United States. National Commission on Excellence in Education. *A Nation at Risk: The Imperative for Educational Reform. A Report to the Nation and the Secretary of Education*. United States Department of Education. Washington, DC: The Commission [Supt. of Docs., US GPO distributor], 1983.

White, E. B., illustrated by Garth Williams, and watercolors by Rosemary Wells. *Charlotte's Web*. Collector's ed., 1st ed. New York: HarperCollins Publishers, 1999.

Wood, Peter. *Drilling through the Core*. Boston: Pioneer Institute for Public Policy Research, 2015.

RESOURCES

Websites, Organizations, and Conferences

Center for Action and Contemplation: Located in Albuquerque, New Mexico, and founded by Richard Rohr, the center seeks to empower individuals in contemplative principles. Many of the center's courses are offered online. CAC.org

Center for Courage & Renewal: Founded by Parker Palmer around the core principles he outlined in his work *The Courage to Teach*, the center offers workshops that embrace reflective practices for both teachers and students. Couragerenewal.org

CMind: The Center for Contemplative Mind in Society hosts an annual interdisciplinary forum for all aspects of research and scholarship on contemplative practices in higher education. Contemplativemind.org

Garrison Institute: The Garrison Institute provides yearly retreats to introduce and deepen participants' understanding of contemplative practices. The institute runs a program called CARE, which seeks to Cultivate Awareness and Resilience in Education. Garrisoninstitute.org

InsightTimer (app): This wonderful app for your phone includes a meditation timer, guided meditations, and even courses. It is well worth exploring this rich resource and even considering using the guided meditations as examples for developing your own practice. Insighttimer.com

International Thomas Merton Society (ITMS): The Thomas Merton Center runs a yearly conference where researchers and scholars share their work as it relates to Merton and the world. Merton.org/ITMS

Inward Bound Mindfulness Education (IBME): This nonprofit program aims to introduce teens to reflective practices through both weekend and weeklong meditation retreats. IBME.info

Kripalu: A retreat center in western Massachusetts, Kripalu runs workshops on meditation throughout the year. The center is rooted in the practice of yoga, and many of these workshops take a yogi's perspective on topics like education and mindfulness. Kripalu.org

Learning & the Brain: This organization "connects educators with the latest research on the brain" and organizes annual conferences, which have more recently included sessions on meditation and mindfulness in the classroom. Learningandthebrain.com

Little Flower Yoga: Based in New York, Little Flower teaches yoga and mindfulness classes in schools and offers training for teachers. Littlefloweryoga.com

Mindful Education: The Association for Mindfulness in Education is a collaborative association of organizations that support reflective practices in schools. Mindfuleducation.com

Mindful Schools: This great nonprofit offers a host of online courses relating to mindfulness and education. They even offer a summer graduate retreat for teachers looking to introduce these practices into their classrooms. Mindfulschools.org

Omega Institute: Each summer the Omega Institute in Rhinebeck, New York, runs a conference bringing together leaders in the field to discuss mindfulness, as well as social and emotional learning. The conference is usually preceded by a weeklong workshop that looks at the specifics of implementing these practices into schools. Eomega.org

Plum Village: A Buddhist monastery founded by Thich Nhat Hanh in southwest France, Plum Village runs a series of year-round programs for teachers connected to the Wake Up Schools movement. Plumvillage.org

INDEX

ABOUT THE AUTHOR

William Meyer has taught history, economics, and humanities in urban and suburban high schools. He has also taught meditation to students of all ages, served as the adviser to student-led meditation clubs, and created a humanities elective for students seeking to incorporate meditation into their rigorous academic lives. He has taught workshops and professional development courses on meditation for other educators and has spoken on meditation and education at retreats and education conferences throughout the country. He is the author of two middle reader novels published by Sleeping Bear Press, as well as *Big Breath*, a guided meditation children's book. He holds a BA from Dartmouth and an MA in education and teaching from Harvard. He is currently completing a PhD from NYU.

BillPMeyer.com

NEW WORLD LIBRARY is dedicated to publishing books and other media that inspire and challenge us to improve the quality of our lives and the world.

We are a socially and environmentally aware company. We recognize that we have an ethical responsibility to our readers, our authors, our staff members, and our planet.

We serve our readers by creating the finest publications possible on personal growth, creativity, spirituality, wellness, and other areas of emerging importance. We serve our authors by working with them to produce and promote quality books that reach a wide audience. We serve New World Library employees with generous benefits, significant profit sharing, and constant encouragement to pursue their most expansive dreams.

Whenever possible, we print our books with soy-based ink on 100 percent postconsumer-waste recycled paper. We power our offices with solar energy and contribute to nonprofit organizations working to make the world a better place for us all.

Our products are available wherever books are sold. Visit our website to download our catalog, subscribe to our e-newsletter, read our blog, and link to authors' websites, videos, and podcasts.

customerservice@newworldlibrary.com
Phone: 415-884-2100 or 800-972-6657
Orders: Ext. 10 • Catalog requests: Ext. 10
Fax: 415-884-2199

www.newworldlibrary.com